Muhammad:

Lasting Resilience Model

Unlocking the Secrets of the Most Influential Life in
History to Master the Ultimate Resilience Model

Dr. Ashi Ezz

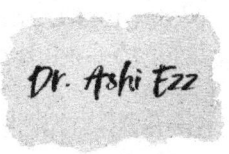

In this book;

Allah: The common name for God in Arabic, similar to Ha-El in Hebrew and Alaha-i in Aramaic. Muslims frequently use the term Allah to refer to God, the one and only.

Prophet Muhammad: The reviver of Islam, was recognized by Michael H. as the most influential figure in history.

The Basmala: A common phrase among Muslims meaning "In the name of God, the Most Gracious, the Most Merciful."

Alhamdulillah: A phrase used by Muslims meaning "All praise is due to God, Lord of all the worlds."

Peace Be Upon Him (PBUH): A phrase used in Islamic tradition to show respect. Muslims say or write it to seek Allah's blessings for the prophet or messenger, and in doing so, receive blessings themselves.

MLRM: It refers to Muhammad's Lasting Resilience Model.

Tawakkul: A common word among Muslims meaning trust in God's plan.

Qadr: A common word among Muslims meaning belief in destiny.

Kaaba: is the most sacred site in Islam, located in Mecca, Saudi Arabia, and serves as the qibla (direction of prayer) for Muslims worldwide.

Contents

Introduction

In the heart of Gaza, amidst the ruins of war and the cries of loss, there stands a mother; a figure who, despite unimaginable grief, embodies a resilience that defies comprehension. Om Ahmed Seyam, a widow, lost her son Ahmed during an Israeli airstrike. Her world, already shadowed by hardship, crumbled further as she searched in vain for his body. Days turned into nights filled with uncertainty, her heart torn between hope and despair, as she feared her son lay buried beneath the rubble of what was once their home.

Yet, in the face of this overwhelming sorrow, Om Ahmed Seyam did not surrender to despair. She now lives in a tent with her four daughters, navigating a life stripped of its comforts and familiarities, yet still carrying the weight of motherhood with unwavering resolve. She exemplifies a spirit of endurance, that challenges us to ask: What fuels such resilience?

Is it faith that binds her to this earth, a belief in something greater that transcends her suffering? Or is it something else; a deeper, almost primal instinct to protect, nurture, and survive? When we see her, and others like her, in the news, their faces etched with the trials of war, we are compelled to wonder: What is behind this unbreakable spirit? Why they keep saying "Alhamdullah" and refer to their beloved Muhammad (peace be upon him), he taught them so, and they move on?!

This question is not just about Om Ahmed Seyam; it is about the countless others who stand resilient in the face of adversity. Their stories were the spark that ignited the writing of this book.

What drives this resilience? Is it faith, a deep-seated belief that suffering is temporary and purpose is eternal? Is it community, the ties that bind people together in mutual support? Or is it something else entirely; a unique blend of these forces, sculpted by context and culture? As we delve into these questions, we begin to uncover the essence of resilience; a quality that, while universal, manifests uniquely in every life it touches. And who is Muhammad?

Who is Muhammad?

Imagine a man who, against all odds, reshaped the moral and spiritual landscape of an entire region; and whose influence continues to resonate with nearly two billion people today. That man is Prophet Muhammad, born around 570 CE in the bustling city of Mecca. Orphaned by the age of six, Muhammad (PBUH) was raised first by his grandfather and then his uncle, growing up in a society steeped in tribal conflicts and polytheistic traditions.

But adversity didn't define him; it refined him. Muhammad (PBUH) became known for his integrity and wisdom, traits that earned him the nickname "Al-Amin," the Trustworthy. At 40 years old, during one of his reflective retreats in the Cave of Hira, something extraordinary happened. He reported a profound encounter with the angel Gabriel, who delivered to him the first revelations of the Quran. This moment was not just a personal awakening; it was the spark that ignited a transformational movement.

Muhammad (PBUH) emerged from that cave with a message both simple and revolutionary: there is only one God, and a life of complete submission to this singular divine authority is the path to true fulfillment. He began sharing these revelations publicly in 613 CE, challenging the deeply ingrained polytheistic beliefs of Meccan society.

Understandably, this didn't sit well with the local power structures. For 13 grueling years, Muhammad (PBUH) and his small but growing group of followers faced intense persecution.

Yet, resilience was his hallmark. To safeguard his followers, he sent some to Abyssinia (modern-day Ethiopia) in 615 CE, seeking refuge under a Christian king known for his justice. Then, in a defining moment of strategic foresight and courage, Muhammad (PBUH) undertook the Hijrah; the migration from Mecca to Medina; in 622 CE. This wasn't just a physical journey but a pivotal turning point that marked the beginning of the Islamic calendar.

In Medina, Muhammad's leadership abilities shone brilliantly. He united feuding tribes under the groundbreaking Constitution of Medina, establishing a pluralistic society based on mutual respect and shared responsibility. This was more than a political maneuver; it was a blueprint for community resilience and ethical governance.

But the challenges were far from over. After eight years of intermittent conflict with the Meccan tribes, Muhammad (PBUH) made a bold move. In 629 CE, he assembled an army of 10,000 followers and marched toward Mecca. Anticipating bloodshed, many braced for the worst. Instead, the conquest was largely peaceful, a testament to Muhammad's strategic acumen and commitment to mercy. By exercising restraint, he transformed former enemies into allies, further solidifying the foundations of a unified Arabian Peninsula.

In 632 CE, shortly after delivering his Farewell Pilgrimage; an address encapsulating his core teachings on justice, equality, and faith; Muhammad (PBUH) passed away. By then, his mission had achieved what many thought impossible: the unification of a fragmented region under the banner of Islam.

The revelations Muhammad (PBUH) received over 23 years comprise the Quran, considered by Muslims to be the literal word of God. But his influence doesn't stop there. His teachings and practices, known as the Sunnah, have been meticulously preserved through Hadith and Sīrah literature. These texts serve as essential guides for Islamic law and personal conduct, extending his legacy far beyond his lifetime.

Prophet Muhammad (PBUH) wasn't just a religious figure; he was a visionary leader, a social reformer, and a paragon of resilience. His life illustrates the profound impact one individual can have when steadfast in purpose and guided by unwavering principles. His journey from an orphaned child to a transformative leader offers timeless lessons on overcoming adversity, the power of faith, and the importance of ethical leadership.

In a world often fraught with division and uncertainty, Muhammad's legacy serves as a compelling reminder of what's possible when one commits fully to a cause greater than oneself. His story isn't merely a chapter in history books; it's a living narrative that continues to inspire and challenge us to strive for a more just and compassionate world.

Prophet Muhammad: A Timeless Role Model

In the quest to understand and cultivate resilience, we could have chosen any number of historical figures, but none come close to embodying the essence of resilience like Prophet Muhammad. Named the most influential person on earth by the renowned historian Michael H. Hart in his book *The 100: A Ranking of the Most Influential Persons in History*, Muhammad's impact is unparalleled. But this title isn't just a reflection of a moment in time; it's a recognition of a legacy that spans over fourteen centuries, touching nearly two billion lives today and countless more across history.

Muhammad's influence is not limited to one sphere of life. He is the only person in history who has demonstrated transformative leadership across personal, organizational, community, and global dimensions. From the way he conducted himself in his private life to the way he led armies and governed a diverse society, Muhammad's teachings and actions offer a blueprint for resilience that transcends time and culture.

Consider this: his companions, numbering over 100,000, meticulously recorded every detail of his life after he became a prophet. This was not merely out of reverence but because they recognized the profound impact his words and actions would have on generations to come. Whether it was something as personal as how to conduct oneself in moments of grief or as public as establishing a just and equitable society, Muhammad (PBUH) provided guidance that was both practical and deeply rooted in ethical principles.

What makes Muhammad's legacy even more compelling is the enduring love and devotion of his followers. Even centuries after his passing, his teachings continue to guide billions of people, influencing how they live, work, and interact with the world. His impact is not just a relic of the past; it's a living force that shapes global cultures and societies.

His influence is unmatched because it is comprehensive. Unlike other historical figures whose impact might be confined to a particular field; be it politics, philosophy, or religion; Muhammad's teachings encompass every aspect of life. From the mundane, such as how to perform daily hygiene, to the profound, like how to build a cohesive and resilient community, his guidance is holistic and all-encompassing.

Moreover, Muhammad's life was a testament to the power of resilience. He faced adversity at every turn; persecution, exile, and even assassination attempts. Yet, through it all, he remained steadfast, never wavering in his mission. His resilience wasn't just about enduring hardships; it was about transforming those hardships into opportunities for growth and learning. This is why his life serves as the ultimate model for resilience, and why the **Muhammad's Lasting Resilience Model (MLRM)** we have developed is not just a theoretical framework, but a living, breathing guide to overcoming the challenges of modern life. Throughout the book, you may notice the story being repeated from different perspectives. This is because a single story can offer many key insights. His stories are rich with lessons learned.

In choosing Muhammad (PBUH) as the model for this book, we are not just looking to the past; we are crafting a vision for the future. His life and teachings offer timeless lessons that are as relevant today as they were over a millennium ago. By studying his resilience, we can build a framework that empowers individuals, organizations, communities, and even nations to thrive in the face of adversity. This is why Muhammad (PBUH) is not just the ideal model for this book; he is the only model that truly captures the essence of lasting resilience.

When we examine the most influential figures in history, a parade of names might come to mind; Alexander the Great, Confucius, Julius Caesar, Napoleon Bonaparte, Mahatma Gandhi, Martin Luther King Jr., and even modern innovators like Steve Jobs. Each of these individuals left an indelible mark on the world, shaping societies, ideologies, and innovations that continue to echo through time. However, when we compare these monumental figures to Prophet Muhammad, we find a profound distinction: Muhammad's influence is not just broad; it is all-encompassing, seamlessly integrating personal transformation, community building, and global impact.

Let's start with Alexander the Great. His military conquests were legendary, carving out one of the largest empires in history. But what happened after his death? His empire fragmented, unable to sustain the unity he imposed. Muhammad, on the other hand, didn't just unify tribes; he laid down principles of governance and justice that have endured for over 1,400 years. His model didn't just conquer lands; it conquered hearts, creating a resilient community that has withstood the test of time.

Now, consider Confucius. His teachings on morality and social harmony have shaped East Asian cultures for millennia. Yet, his influence remained largely regional. Muhammad's teachings, however, transcended geography, ethnicity, and time, creating a global community bound by shared values; a community that today numbers nearly 2 billion people. While Confucius provided a moral framework, Muhammad (PBUH) offered a comprehensive blueprint for life, one that continues to guide billions in every aspect of their existence.

Even the modern icons; Gandhi, King, Jobs; while transformative, had their influence limited by time and scope. Gandhi's nonviolent resistance inspired movements across the world, yet his influence was primarily tied to the political context of colonial India. Martin Luther King Jr.'s fight for civil rights reshaped America, but its impact, though profound, was largely confined to the struggle for racial equality in the U.S. Steve Jobs revolutionized technology, but his influence, too, is tied to a specific domain. Muhammad, however, was not confined to any one sphere. His teachings addressed every facet of life, from the spiritual to the practical, providing a model for resilience that is as relevant today as it was centuries ago.

What makes Muhammad (PBUH) truly unparalleled is the integration of his influence across all levels of human experience. He wasn't just a spiritual leader or a political strategist; he was both, and more. His life offered guidance on everything from personal conduct to statecraft, from how to handle grief to how to govern justly. His companions recorded every detail of his life, creating a rich tapestry of wisdom that has been studied and followed for over a millennium.

The meticulous documentation of his life by over 100,000 companions is itself a testament to the profound impact he had on those around him. They recorded not just his teachings, but his actions, his decisions, his responses to the challenges of life. This level of detail is unparalleled and provides an exhaustive resource for anyone seeking to understand and emulate his model of resilience.

And here's the clincher: while other figures have left legacies that required reinterpretation or adaptation over time, Muhammad's teachings have remained consistently relevant. His approach to resilience; whether personal, organizational, or communal; is timeless. It's a blueprint that doesn't need updating because it was never confined to the specifics of any one era or culture. It's universal, and it's eternal.

while history is filled with influential figures, none have matched the breadth, depth, and lasting impact of Muhammad. His life and teachings offer a model for resilience that is not only comprehensive but also enduring. Whether guiding individuals through personal challenges, leading communities, or promoting global peace, Muhammad's legacy is the ultimate blueprint for resilience. It's a model that has stood the test of time and continues to provide guidance for millions today, making it the most complete and lasting example of resilience in human history.

The life of Prophet Muhammad (PBUH) provides a rich foundation for understanding and cultivating resilience. His experiences of adversity, personal loss, and societal challenges reveal timeless principles that remain relevant across cultures and contexts. His example offers practical guidance on how to navigate life's challenges with grace, integrity, and unwavering strength.

What is Resilience?

Resilience is more than just bouncing back from challenges; it's about thriving in the face of adversity. In clear, relatable terms, resilience means the capacity to recover quickly from difficulties and to adapt well to change. In our contemporary world, characterized by rapid uncertainty, constant change, and global crises, resilience becomes an indispensable trait. It's the ability to navigate through the stormy waters of life with a sense of purpose and composure, emerging not just intact but stronger.

Purpose of the Book

This book isn't a religious text; it's about delving into meticulously documented historical records and applying structured, logical analysis and system thinking to build a model of resilience. We've tapped into a range of techniques widely recognized in the market, from cognitive behavioral approaches to adaptive leadership strategies, to distill timeless principles from the life of Muhammad. This isn't about faith alone; it's about extracting practical, actionable wisdom from history and aligning it with the best of what modern resilience theory has to offer. We're bridging the gap between historical insight and contemporary application, making this model both relevant and transformative.

This book aims to provide a practical guide to building resilience through the MLRM, inspired by the life of Prophet Muhammad. Drawing from classical Islamic sources, this book will offer actionable strategies for developing resilience in various facets of life. It's not merely about surviving the storms but about leveraging them to build a more robust and fulfilling life.

Sources and Methodology

To underpin the MLRM, this book draws from classical Islamic texts such as *Ar-Raheeq Al-Makhtum* (The Sealed Nectar), *Ash-Shifa* (The Healing), *Al-Shamā'il al-Muhammadiyya* (The Characteristics of Muhammad), *Al-Sirah al-Nabawiyyah* (The Prophetic Biography); and more. These sources provide a comprehensive view of Prophet Muhammad's life, offering insights into his moral, spiritual, emotional, and social resilience. The methodology involves a synthesis of these classical sources with modern principles of resilience to offer a framework that is both timeless and applicable to contemporary challenges.

Introduction to the Muhammad's Lasting Resilience Model (MLRM)

The MLRM is built on four foundational pillars:

1. **Moral and Ethical Resilience**: This pillar draws inspiration from the Prophet's unwavering commitment to truth and justice. It emphasizes the significance of maintaining integrity and ethical conduct, even when faced with significant challenges. By anchoring ourselves in strong moral principles, we can navigate adversity with clarity and purpose.

2. **Spiritual Resilience**: Inspired by the Prophet's profound spiritual connection and trust in Allah, this pillar highlights the role of faith and spiritual practices in overcoming difficulties. Spiritual resilience involves cultivating a deep sense of trust and inner strength, which provides a source of comfort and guidance during turbulent times.

3. **Emotional and Psychological Resilience**: The Prophet's life, marked by personal loss, persecution, and betrayal, showcases his ability to maintain emotional balance and mental fortitude. This pillar focuses on strategies for managing emotions, developing patience, and fostering mental well-being, helping us to remain steadfast and composed in the face of challenges.

4. **Social and Community Resilience**: Prophet Muhammad's life exemplifies the importance of community support and collective responsibility. This pillar explores the role of social connections and communal support in building resilience, emphasizing the power of mutual assistance and shared responsibility in overcoming difficulties.

What to Expect

This book is structured to provide both theoretical insights and practical tools. Each chapter employs system thinking approach to explore the key components that shape the MLRM, offering reflections, real-life applications, and actionable strategies. Readers can expect to gain a holistic understanding of resilience and how to apply these principles to their own lives, drawing inspiration from the life of one of history's greatest role models.

Through this blend of historical wisdom and practical application, this book aims to equip readers with the tools to build lasting resilience, helping them navigate the complexities of modern life with strength and purpose.

Chapter 1: Embracing Change

Cultivating an Adaptive Mindset

In a world where the only constant is change, an adaptive mindset isn't just a luxury; it's a necessity. Adaptability serves as the cornerstone of resilience, allowing us to navigate through life's inevitable twists and turns. The capacity to adapt determines whether we merely survive or thrive amidst the chaos of a fast-changing environment.

1.1 Understanding the Power of Adaptability

Adaptability is crucial because it empowers us to respond to unforeseen challenges with agility and creativity. It's the mental flexibility that enables us to pivot our strategies when the old ways no longer work. In a fast-paced world, adaptability ensures that we don't become rigid in our thinking or actions. Instead, it opens the door to innovation, allowing us to reframe problems as opportunities for growth. Without adaptability, we risk stagnation, clinging to outdated methods and mindsets that no longer serve us.

The Science of Adaptability

From a psychological and neurological perspective, adaptability is rooted in our brain's ability to rewire itself, a concept known as neuroplasticity. This ability to form new neural connections underpins our capacity to learn and adjust to new circumstances. When we encounter change, our brain evaluates the new information and experiences, integrating them into our existing mental frameworks. This process is not just about coping with change but thriving in it, as our brain evolves to meet the demands of new realities. By cultivating an adaptive mindset, we enhance our cognitive flexibility, improving our capacity to handle stress, solve problems, and ultimately, build resilience.

1.2 Lessons from the Prophet's Life

The life of Prophet Muhammad (PBUH) offers profound lessons in adaptability, showcasing how an adaptive mindset can lead to extraordinary outcomes. His ability to embrace change and guide his followers through uncertainty is a testament to the power of resilience.

Muhammad (PBUH) stands as the ultimate master of adaptation, unmatched in history. Consider this: at the age of 40, his voice emerged in opposition to virtually everyone around him. He wasn't just fighting local resistance; his very existence was seen as a threat to the established social, economic, and political order. People wanted him silenced, not just because of his message, but because of what that message represented; a profound shift in power, belief, and structure. His opponents had everything to lose; financially, psychologically, socially; if his teachings took root.

In the last ten years of his life, based in Medina, Muhammad (PBUH) entered into a war every single year to defend his mission. Let that sink in: every year, a battle, a challenge that could easily have broken anyone else. But it wasn't just warfare. The other daily struggles he faced over the 23 years after his first revelation were the kind that most would consider "life-ending" challenges. Any one of them could have been the final straw for another leader, but Muhammad (PBUH) was different. When most would throw up their hands and say, "I'm too old for this,"

Muhammad (PBUH) adapted, continuously refining his strategy, approach, and even his messaging.

What sets Muhammad (PBUH) apart is not just his resilience in surviving these challenges but his capacity to build something enduring from them. He didn't just defend his message; he expanded it into a global movement. He didn't just push through adversity; he thrived, building a new social order. And the key? He cloned his vision into each of his companions, ensuring that his mission would outlast him. His adaptability wasn't just a survival mechanism; it was a deliberate strategy to grow and solidify a lasting legacy.

Consider the evidence: each of his closest companions took on the role of expanding his message; Abu Bakr became the first caliph, solidifying political stability; Ali led with wisdom and justice; and Umar spread the message across vast territories. These were not random followers; they were trained to carry forth the vision, ensuring it wasn't just Muhammad's message, but *their* message too. This was no accident; it was the result of relentless adaptation, an evolution that was deeply authentic and grounded in the truth of what he believed.

Leading Through Change

Prophet Muhammad's leadership during times of change and uncertainty is another profound example of adaptability. His ability to manage transitions and guide his community through difficult times was rooted in his deep understanding of human nature and his unwavering faith in divine wisdom. Three stories from his life illustrate this beautifully:

The Revelation at Cave Hira: The first revelation in the Cave of Hira was a transformative moment in the Prophet's life, marking the beginning of his prophethood. Initially, the experience was overwhelming, filling him with fear and uncertainty. However, with the support of his wife Khadijah and the wise counsel of Waraqa ibn Nawfal, the Prophet embraced his new role as the Messenger of God. This pivotal moment required him to adopt an adaptive mindset, accepting the monumental change in his life and the responsibilities it entailed. His ability to adapt to this new reality laid the foundation for his mission and the eventual rise of Islam.

The Migration to Medina (Hijra): The Hijra, or migration to Medina, was a critical turning point for the early Muslim community. Leaving behind his homeland, Prophet Muhammad (PBUH) had to adapt to a new environment, build alliances with unfamiliar tribes, and establish a new social order in Medina. This required not only physical relocation but also a mental and emotional adjustment. The Prophet's ability to lead his followers through this transition, turning a moment of crisis into an opportunity for community building, demonstrates a mindset deeply rooted in resilience and adaptability. His leadership during the Hijra is a powerful example of transforming adversity into growth.

The Adaptation to Medina's Climate: When the early Muslims made their way to Medina, they faced an environment vastly different from their familiar Meccan climate. The harsh, unfamiliar weather led to illness among some of the emigrants. Prophet Muhammad, embodying both wisdom and practical leadership, took decisive action. He not only educated his followers on how to better cope with the new climate but also guided them in adapting their practices to fit Medina's agricultural conditions. This proactive approach exemplifies how true resilience involves not just enduring change, but actively transforming it into a source of growth and opportunity.

The Change in Qibla: Another significant moment of change was the alteration of the Qibla, the direction of prayer. Initially, Muslims were instructed to face Jerusalem, but after the migration to Medina, the direction was changed to the Kaaba in Mecca. This shift was not merely a physical reorientation but also a profound symbolic change, one that required the Muslim community to adapt to a new directive. The Prophet's acceptance and communication of this change to his followers underscored his adaptability and trust in divine guidance. This incident highlights the importance of embracing change with resilience and faith, trusting in the wisdom behind new paths.

The Establishment of the Call to Prayer (Adhan): In Medina, a new challenge emerged: how to call the faithful to prayer in a way that would be both effective and distinctive. Initially, there were various proposals; bells, fires, and other methods; but none felt quite right. Then, inspired by a divine vision, Prophet Muhammad (PBUH) introduced the Adhan, or call to prayer. This innovative approach didn't just address the practical need for a prayer call; it revolutionized the practice, aligning it with the community's needs and cultural context. The Adhan's introduction was not merely a change in ritual but a strategic adaptation that demonstrated how openness to new ideas can lead to profound and lasting impact.

Changing the Treaty of Hudaybiyyah's Terms: The Treaty of Hudaybiyyah presented a situation where Prophet Muhammad (PBUH) accepted terms that seemed unfavorable at first glance, such as the omission of his title "Messenger of God" in the treaty's text. To the untrained eye, it might have appeared as a concession. However, this strategic flexibility was rooted in a deeper understanding of the broader picture. By adapting to these terms, the Prophet prioritized long-term peace and strategic advantage over immediate gains. His willingness to adjust expectations in the pursuit of a greater good highlights the essence of resilience: recognizing that embracing change can lead to transformative benefits that far exceed initial setbacks.

Adaptability is not just a trait; it is a mindset that must be cultivated and nurtured. The examples from Prophet Muhammad's life illustrate how embracing change and remaining open to new possibilities can lead to remarkable outcomes. By fostering an adaptive mindset, we prepare ourselves to face the uncertainties of life with resilience, turning challenges into opportunities for growth and transformation. As we embark on this journey of cultivating adaptability, we draw inspiration from the timeless lessons of the Prophet, learning to navigate change with grace, wisdom, and unwavering strength.

Key Takeaways:

- **Change as a Constant:** The Prophet Muhammad's life, particularly his migration to Medina, illustrates that change is an inevitable and essential part of life. Embracing change, rather than resisting it, is crucial for growth and resilience.
- **Adaptation Over Time:** Just as the Prophet introduced the Adhan as a new way to call believers to prayer, we must be willing to adapt our practices to new circumstances. This flexibility allows us to maintain our core values while adjusting to new realities.

- **Strategic Acceptance:** The Prophet's acceptance of the unfavorable terms in the Treaty of Hudaybiyyah teaches us that sometimes, embracing change requires us to see the bigger picture and make temporary sacrifices for long-term benefits.

Reflection: Like a tree bending in the wind to avoid breaking, we must learn to adapt to life's challenges. Embrace change as an opportunity for growth, and strategically adapt to ensure long-term resilience.

1.3 Developing Your Adaptive Skills

Cultivating an adaptive mindset is akin to building a muscle. It requires deliberate practice, consistent effort, and a willingness to step out of your comfort zone. In this section, we'll explore practical techniques to help you welcome change, develop cognitive flexibility, and overcome resistance; both internal and external; to build the resilience needed in today's ever-changing world.

Welcoming Change

Embracing Uncertainty as a Catalyst for Growth: The first step in developing adaptability is shifting your perspective on change. Instead of viewing change as a disruption, start seeing it as an opportunity for growth. This mindset shift involves embracing uncertainty and recognizing that every change, whether positive or negative, carries the potential for new experiences, learning, and self-improvement.

Techniques for Fostering a Change-Embracing Mindset

- **Mindful Acceptance**: Practice mindfulness to stay present and grounded when faced with change. Instead of reacting impulsively to new circumstances, take a moment to observe your thoughts and emotions without judgment. This practice helps you approach change with a calm, open mind, reducing fear and anxiety.

- **Reframing**: Reframe challenges as opportunities. When a change occurs, ask yourself, "What can I learn from this?" or "How can this situation help me grow?" By reframing your thoughts, you shift your focus from what you might lose to what you could gain, making change less intimidating.

- **Exposure to New Experiences**: Regularly expose yourself to new experiences, whether it's learning a new skill, traveling to an unfamiliar place, or engaging in diverse social activities. These experiences build your comfort with uncertainty and prepare you to handle bigger changes with greater ease.

Flexibility in Thinking

Cognitive Flexibility is The Key to Adaptability: Cognitive flexibility; the ability to shift your thinking and adapt your approach; is essential for navigating change. This skill allows you to see problems from different perspectives, adjust your strategies as needed, and remain open to new ideas. Developing cognitive flexibility requires practice, but it can be cultivated through specific exercises.

Exercises to Enhance Cognitive Flexibility

- **Perspective-Taking**: Regularly challenge yourself to view situations from different angles. For example, when facing a problem, think about how someone with a different background or mindset might approach it. This exercise helps you break out of rigid thinking patterns and develop a more adaptable mindset.
- **Mental Contrasting**: Visualize both the positive and negative aspects of a potential change. By mentally contrasting the best and worst outcomes, you prepare your mind for a range of possibilities, making it easier to adjust your approach as circumstances evolve.
- **Brainstorming Alternatives**: When faced with a decision or problem, brainstorm multiple solutions or approaches, even if some seem unconventional. This practice encourages creative thinking and helps you become more comfortable with exploring and adopting new strategies.

Overcoming Resistance

Identifying the Roots of Resistance: Resistance to change often stems from fear; fear of the unknown, fear of failure, or fear of losing control. To overcome this resistance, it's crucial to identify its roots and address them head-on. Resistance can also be external, coming from social or organizational pressures. Developing adaptability involves both internal reflection and external negotiation.

Strategies for Breaking Down Resistance

- **Self-Awareness**: Increase your self-awareness by regularly reflecting on your thoughts and feelings about change. Identify any fears or anxieties that may be holding you back. Once you're aware of these barriers, you can begin to address them through positive self-talk, goal-setting, or seeking support from others.

- **Incremental Change**: Start with small, manageable changes rather than attempting a major overhaul all at once. By gradually exposing yourself to change, you reduce resistance and build confidence in your ability to adapt. This approach also allows you to learn and adjust without feeling overwhelmed.

- **Communicating the Benefits**: When dealing with external resistance, whether in a work environment or social setting, focus on clearly communicating the benefits of the change. Help others see the positive outcomes and the long-term advantages, making the case for why adaptation is necessary and beneficial.

1.4 Reflect and Apply

Developing an adaptive mindset is not just about learning new skills; it's about integrating them into your daily life. This section will guide you through reflecting on your current approach to change and provide actionable steps for making adaptability a part of your routine.

Personal Reflection

Assessing Your Current Adaptability: Take a moment to reflect on how you currently handle change. Do you welcome it, or does it fill you with anxiety? How do you react when things don't go according to plan? Reflecting on your past experiences with change can provide valuable insights into your current level of adaptability.

Guiding Questions for Reflection

- When was the last time you faced a significant change? How did you handle it?
- What emotions do you typically feel when confronted with change?
- How often do you seek out new experiences or challenge yourself to try something different?
- In what areas of your life do you feel most resistant to change?

Action Steps

Incorporating Adaptability into Daily Life: Building adaptability requires consistent practice. Here are practical steps you can take to make adaptability a part of your everyday routine, emphasizing small, achievable goals that gradually build your resilience.

1. **Set Micro-Challenges**: Regularly set small challenges that push you out of your comfort zone. This could be as simple as trying a new hobby, taking a different route to work, or initiating a conversation with someone new. These micro-challenges build your adaptability muscle by gradually increasing your tolerance for change.
2. **Practice Flexible Thinking Daily**: Dedicate a few minutes each day to exercises that enhance cognitive flexibility. For instance, at the end of the day, reflect on a situation where you could have

approached things differently. Consider alternative perspectives or strategies you could have used.

3. **Create a Change-Positive Environment**: Surround yourself with people, resources, and environments that encourage adaptability. Engage with books, podcasts, or communities that emphasize growth and change. By immersing yourself in a culture of adaptability, you reinforce the mindset in your own life.

4. **Track Your Progress**: Keep a journal to track your experiences with change. Note the challenges you faced, how you responded, and what you learned. This practice not only helps you see your growth over time but also reinforces the habit of reflecting on and learning from change.

CHAPTER GEM ELEMENTS

❖ **Embrace the Uncertainty of Change**: Recognize change as a constant and develop an adaptive mindset that sees uncertainty as an opportunity for growth.

❖ **Strategic Adaptation**: Employ strategic thinking to adapt to changing circumstances while maintaining core values and objectives.

❖ **Reframe Your Perspective**: Shift from a fear-based view of change to a perspective that embraces it as a catalyst for innovation and progress.

❖ **Adaptation Over Time**: Understand that adaptation is an ongoing process, requiring continuous reflection and adjustment.

❖ **Strategic Acceptance**: Accept what cannot be changed and focus energy on areas where impact is possible.

Chapter 2: Mastering Your Emotions

Building Emotional Intelligence

Emotions are powerful forces that shape our thoughts, actions, and relationships. Mastering them is not about suppression but about understanding, channeling, and regulating them in ways that enhance our resilience and well-being. In this chapter, we delve into the critical aspects of emotional regulation and intelligence, drawing lessons from the life of Prophet Muhammad (PBUH) to illustrate the profound impact of emotional mastery on resilience.

2.1 The Importance of Emotional Regulation

Why Emotional Control is Key: Emotional regulation is the ability to manage and respond to our emotions in a healthy, balanced manner. It is not about ignoring or denying our emotions but about controlling how we express them. In the context of resilience, emotional regulation is essential because it allows us to maintain composure during stressful situations, make rational decisions, and avoid actions driven by impulsive reactions.

Imagine standing in the middle of a storm, with strong winds and rain battering you from all directions. Without emotional regulation, you might find yourself overwhelmed, unable to think clearly or act effectively. But with it, you're like a ship with a strong anchor, able to withstand the storm without being swept away. Emotional regulation provides that anchor, ensuring that even in the most challenging circumstances, you remain grounded and focused.

The Role of Emotional Intelligence: Emotional intelligence (EQ) goes beyond just controlling our emotions; it involves recognizing, understanding, and managing not only our own emotions but also those of others. High emotional intelligence enables us to navigate social complexities, build stronger relationships, and make better decisions under pressure.

EQ is composed of several key elements:

1. **Self-Awareness**: The ability to recognize and understand your own emotions.
2. **Self-Regulation**: The ability to control or redirect disruptive emotions and impulses.
3. **Motivation**: A passion for work that goes beyond money or status, driven by inner ambitions.
4. **Empathy**: The ability to understand and share the feelings of others.
5. **Social Skills**: The ability to manage relationships and build networks.

In resilience, EQ allows us to manage stress, remain optimistic, and foster a supportive environment, all of which are crucial in overcoming adversity. Emotional intelligence helps us to respond rather than react, ensuring that our actions are aligned with our values and long-term goals.

2.2 The Prophet's Emotional Mastery

The Power of Positive Affirmation (Husn al-Dhann and Positive Mindset)

Prophet Muhammad's life provides timeless examples of emotional mastery based in a core principle. The concept of Husn al-Dhann (having a good opinion of God and others) aligns with the idea that maintaining a positive outlook, even in challenging times, shapes one's reality. This is about rewiring the self to stay optimistic, believing that after every difficulty, ease will follow, as mentioned in the Qur'an (94:6).

Husn al-Dhann, or the power of positive thinking, emphasizes maintaining a hopeful and optimistic outlook. This is crucial for resilience, as it encourages individuals to see challenges as opportunities for growth and to believe that ease follows hardship. This aligns with cognitive behavioral strategies that focus on reframing negative thoughts and maintaining a positive mindset.

The idea of maintaining a positive internal dialogue and avoiding the drain of negative energy. Emotional mastery is not just about controlling negative emotions but also about fostering positive ones.

Through his experiences, we can learn how to navigate our own emotional landscapes with wisdom and grace.

Navigating Personal Loss

Life is filled with moments of loss, and how we handle these moments defines our resilience. The Prophet Muhammad (PBUH) experienced profound personal losses, including the passing of his beloved wife Khadijah and several of his children. Each instance of loss was a test of his emotional strength, and his responses offer deep insights into emotional intelligence.

The Death of His Son, Ibrahim: One of the most poignant examples of the Prophet's emotional mastery is the death of his young son, Ibrahim. The Prophet's love for his son was deep, and his grief was palpable. Yet, even in his sorrow, he exhibited profound emotional regulation. He allowed himself to feel and express his grief; "The eyes shed tears and the heart is grieved, but we will not say anything except what pleases our Lord." These words, recorded in "Al-Shamā'il al-Muhammadiyya," reflect his ability to hold space for his emotions while maintaining a sense of peace and acceptance. This balance between feeling and restraint is a hallmark of emotional intelligence, where one acknowledges pain but doesn't let it lead to despair or bitterness.

Controlling Anger and Practicing Forgiveness

Anger is one of the most challenging emotions to regulate, often leading to destructive actions if not managed properly. The Prophet Muhammad (PBUH) demonstrated exceptional control over his anger, using it constructively or transforming it into forgiveness.

The Treaty of Hudaybiyyah: During the negotiations of the Treaty of Hudaybiyyah, the Prophet faced a situation where emotions could have easily escalated into conflict. The terms of the treaty seemed unfavorable to the Muslims, causing frustration and disappointment among his followers. However, the Prophet remained composed, understanding the long-term benefits of peace over immediate emotional satisfaction. His emotional control, coupled with strategic foresight, turned what seemed like a setback into a significant victory. This incident, documented in "Al-Sirah al-Nabawiyyah," highlights the importance of patience and emotional regulation in achieving lasting success.

The Incident of the Slur: Another powerful example of emotional mastery is the incident involving his wife Aisha, who was falsely accused of infidelity. The emotional turmoil this situation caused was immense, affecting not only the Prophet but the entire community. Instead of reacting impulsively or out of anger, the Prophet sought divine guidance and maintained his composure. His restraint during this period of intense pressure, and his eventual vindication of Aisha through divine revelation, as recounted in "Ash-Shifa," exemplifies the strength that comes from emotional intelligence. The ability to remain calm, seek the truth, and act justly despite personal pain is a profound lesson in managing emotions under stress.

The Patience with the Bedouin's Disrespect: Imagine this: a Bedouin approaches Prophet Muhammad, yanking his cloak with a harsh demand for charity. Instead of reacting with indignation or annoyance, the Prophet responds with serene composure, fulfilling the request with kindness. This moment is a masterclass in emotional intelligence; rather than letting anger or disrespect dictate his response, he harnesses his inner calm to turn an abrasive encounter into an opportunity for grace. His ability to manage his emotions and act with benevolence, despite the provocation, underscores a profound emotional intelligence that transforms potential conflict into a moment of teaching and humanity. Source: *Al-Sirah al-Nabawiyyah*

The Prophet's Restraint in Personal Insults: Throughout his life, Prophet Muhammad (PBUH) faced numerous insults and mockery from adversaries. Yet, time and again, he demonstrated an unwavering control over his emotions. Rather than letting personal attacks provoke a retaliatory response, he maintained his patience and dignity, understanding that his reaction; or lack thereof; set a powerful example for his followers. His restraint was not a sign of weakness but a deliberate choice to embody the virtues of patience and composure. This deep-seated emotional intelligence allowed him to rise above petty grievances, focusing instead on the broader mission and impact of his teachings. Source: *Dalail al-Khayra*

The Prophet's Reaction to the Hypocrites: In the face of hypocrites spreading false rumors and undermining the unity of the Muslim community in Medina, Prophet Muhammad (PBUH) chose a path of strategic patience and wisdom. Instead of immediate public confrontation or expulsion, he allowed time for their true intentions to surface, addressing the issue with a measured and thoughtful approach. This tactic reflects an advanced level of emotional intelligence in leadership; managing one's emotions and actions to outmaneuver deceit and maintain community cohesion. His approach demonstrated that effective leadership often involves navigating challenges with calm resolve and allowing the natural course of events to reveal the truth. Source: *Kitab al-Samarkandiyya*

Key Takeaways:

- **Emotional Mastery:** The Prophet's calm response to the Bedouin's disrespect shows that true strength lies in mastering our emotions, not letting them control us. Emotional intelligence is about responding with wisdom, not reacting impulsively.

- **Patience in Adversity:** When facing insults or opposition, as the Prophet did with the hypocrites, it's essential to maintain composure. By managing emotions, you can navigate challenges more effectively and maintain your moral integrity.
- **Restraint as Strength:** The Prophet's decision not to retaliate against personal insults reflects the power of restraint. By controlling anger and choosing forgiveness, we can rise above the situation and maintain inner peace.

Reflection: Emotional intelligence is not about suppressing feelings but about understanding and managing them effectively. Like the Prophet, practice patience and composure to build resilience in the face of emotional challenges.

Mastering your emotions is a lifelong journey that requires continual reflection and practice. By understanding and applying the principles of emotional intelligence, you can enhance your resilience and navigate life's challenges with greater ease and effectiveness.

2.3 Enhancing Emotional Intelligence

Emotional intelligence is not just about understanding your emotions; it's about actively cultivating the skills to manage and utilize them in ways that enhance your life and relationships. To develop this crucial aspect of resilience, we can draw on several practical techniques, each of which is deeply rooted in both psychological principles and the examples from the life of Prophet Muhammad.

Mindfulness and Presence

The Role of Mindfulness in Emotional Regulation: Mindfulness is the practice of being fully present in the moment, observing your thoughts and feelings without judgment. This heightened awareness allows you to notice emotions as they arise, giving you the space to choose how to respond rather than reacting impulsively.

The Prophet Muhammad's emotional mastery, as seen in the examples from his life, reflects a deep presence and mindfulness. For instance, during the Treaty of Hudaybiyyah, his ability to remain calm and focused, despite the emotionally charged atmosphere, demonstrates the power of mindfulness. By staying present, he was able to navigate a difficult situation with wisdom and foresight.

Practical Mindfulness Exercise: To cultivate mindfulness, start with a simple breathing exercise:

1. **Find a Quiet Space**: Sit comfortably and close your eyes.
2. **Focus on Your Breath**: Pay attention to your breathing, noticing the sensation of the air entering and leaving your body.
3. **Observe Your Thoughts and Emotions**: As you breathe, observe any thoughts or emotions that arise. Don't try to change them; just notice them.
4. **Return to Your Breath**: If your mind wanders, gently bring your focus back to your breath.

Practicing this for just a few minutes each day can significantly enhance your emotional awareness and control, much like how the Prophet maintained his composure in challenging situations.

Journaling for Emotional Clarity

Understanding Emotions Through Writing: Journaling is a powerful tool for emotional clarity. By writing down your thoughts and feelings, you can track your emotional triggers, understand your responses, and identify patterns in your behavior. This practice helps you move from emotional confusion to clarity, making it easier to regulate your emotions.

Consider the Prophet's reflection after the death of his son, Ibrahim. His ability to articulate his grief; "The eyes shed tears and the heart is grieved, but we will not say anything except what pleases our Lord"; demonstrates the power of clearly expressing emotions. Journaling offers a similar opportunity for you to process and understand your feelings.

Journaling Exercise

1. **Daily Reflection**: At the end of each day, take 10 minutes to write about the emotions you experienced. What triggered them? How did you respond?
2. **Identify Patterns**: After a week, review your entries. Look for patterns; do certain situations or people consistently trigger strong emotions?
3. **Plan for Improvement**: Based on your observations, set goals for how you want to manage these emotions in the future.

This practice not only enhances emotional intelligence but also helps you apply the Prophet's approach to emotional mastery in your own life.

Reframing Emotions

Reframing is a cognitive technique that involves changing the way you interpret emotional experiences. Instead of seeing an emotion as purely negative, reframing helps you view it as an opportunity for growth or learning.

For example, when Prophet Muhammad (PBUH) faced the false accusations against Aisha, he could have been consumed by anger or despair. Instead, he reframed the situation by seeking divine guidance, viewing the trial as a test of patience and faith. This reframing allowed him to manage his emotions constructively, ultimately leading to a just outcome.

Reframing Exercise

1. **Identify a Challenging Emotion**: Think of a recent situation where you experienced a strong negative emotion.
2. **Explore Alternative Interpretations**: Ask yourself, "What can I learn from this emotion? How can this experience help me grow?"
3. **Write a New Narrative**: Write down a new interpretation of the event that emphasizes positive aspects, such as personal growth, increased resilience, or deeper understanding.

By practicing reframing, you can transform negative emotions into valuable insights, much like the Prophet turned challenging situations into opportunities for spiritual and emotional growth.

2.4 Reflect and Apply

Developing emotional intelligence requires ongoing reflection and intentional practice. The following steps will help you assess and enhance your emotional regulation skills, drawing on the techniques discussed above.

Personal Reflection

Take some time to reflect on your current emotional regulation abilities. Consider the following questions:

- How do you typically respond to emotional triggers? Do you react impulsively, or do you take time to process your emotions?
- Are there certain emotions that you struggle to manage effectively?
- How does your emotional regulation impact your relationships and decision-making?

Reflecting on these questions will help you identify areas for improvement and set the stage for enhancing your emotional intelligence.

Action Steps

To develop your emotional intelligence, incorporate the following practical steps into your daily routine:

1. **Mindfulness Practice**: Dedicate 5-10 minutes each day to mindfulness meditation. This will help you become more aware of your emotions and improve your ability to regulate them.
2. **Daily Journaling**: Spend a few minutes each evening journaling about your emotions. This will help you track your emotional triggers, understand your responses, and identify patterns.
3. **Cognitive Reframing**: When faced with a challenging emotion, practice reframing the situation to see it in a more positive light. Over time, this will help you develop a more resilient mindset.
4. **Regular Reflection**: Set aside time each week to reflect on your emotional experiences and how you managed them. This will help you continually improve your emotional regulation skills.
5. **The Role of Social Support**: Encouraging a positive community atmosphere can prevent negativity from spreading and reinforce mutual support.
6. **Additional Focus**: Integrating positive affirmations into daily practices, as well as encouraging others to do the same.

By integrating these practices into your life, you can enhance your emotional intelligence, leading to greater resilience, better relationships, and a more fulfilling life. Just as the Prophet Muhammad (PBUH) demonstrated extraordinary emotional mastery, you too can develop the skills to navigate life's emotional challenges with wisdom and grace.

CHAPTER GEM ELEMENTS

❖ **Emotional Regulation Through Reflection**: Use self-reflection to manage and regulate emotions, preventing them from becoming obstacles to resilience.

❖ **Patience as Emotional Mastery**: Cultivate patience as a key to mastering emotional responses, especially in the face of adversity.

❖ **Seek Divine Guidance in Emotional Turmoil**: In moments of emotional distress, seek spiritual guidance to find peace and clarity.

❖ **Restraint as Strength**: Recognize restraint as a powerful tool in managing emotions and maintaining control in difficult situations.

Chapter 3: Strength in Connections

The Role of Social Support

In the tapestry of human resilience, social connections are the threads that bind us together, providing strength, support, and a sense of belonging. Our ability to navigate life's challenges is profoundly influenced by the relationships we cultivate and the communities we build. As we explore; in this chapter, the role of social support in fostering resilience, we'll draw lessons from the life of Prophet Muhammad, whose approach to community building offers timeless insights into the power of connection.

3.1 Why Social Bonds Matter

The Power of Support Networks: At the core of resilience lies the ability to withstand adversity, and few things bolster this ability more effectively than strong social connections. When faced with life's inevitable trials, having a network of supportive relationships can make the difference between succumbing to stress and thriving in the face of challenges. Social bonds provide emotional support, practical assistance, and a sense of shared purpose, all of which are crucial for maintaining mental and emotional well-being.

Research in psychology consistently underscores the importance of these networks. Studies show that individuals with strong social ties are more likely to experience lower levels of stress, recover more quickly from illness, and have a higher overall life satisfaction. These connections act as a buffer against life's difficulties, offering comfort in times of need and celebrating successes together.

Prophet Muhammad's life offers profound examples of how social support can fortify resilience. Whether through the bonds of brotherhood he fostered between the Muhajirun and Ansar or the alliances he built through the Pledge of Aqabah, the Prophet demonstrated that collective strength arises from the unity and cooperation of individuals.

Environmental Impact: The environment in which we live significantly influences our resilience. Our surroundings, including the people we interact with, the norms we follow, and the values we uphold, shape our capacity to adapt and thrive. A supportive environment fosters resilience by providing safety, stability, and a sense of belonging. Conversely, a toxic environment can erode resilience, leading to feelings of isolation, stress, and vulnerability.

The Prophet's establishment of the Charter of Medina is a powerful illustration of how shaping a positive environment can enhance communal resilience. By creating a social contract that promoted mutual respect and cooperation among diverse groups, the Prophet ensured that the community in Medina became a nurturing environment where people of different backgrounds could thrive together.

3.2 The Prophet's Approach to Community Building

Prophet Muhammad's leadership in community building was rooted in principles of inclusivity, mutual support, and shared responsibility. His efforts to create cohesive, resilient communities provide valuable lessons for building strong social networks today.

The Gathering at Dar al-Arqam

In the nascent days of Islam, when Mecca was a hotbed of hostility, the Prophet Muhammad (PBUH) established Dar al-Arqam as a clandestine sanctuary for his followers. Within the walls of this secret haven, early Muslims found not only spiritual guidance but also a profound sense of community. This gathering was more than a meeting place; it was a lifeline. It provided a critical refuge from the storm of oppression, demonstrating the indispensable role of social support in nurturing resilience. The gathering at Dar al-Arqam epitomizes how a supportive network can be a bastion of strength when facing adversity.

The Charter of Medina

One of the most significant examples of the Prophet's community-building efforts is the Charter of Medina. After migrating to Medina, the Prophet faced the challenge of uniting a diverse population that included Muslims, Jews, and various Arab tribes. To create harmony and ensure the community's resilience, he established the Charter of Medina; a social contract that outlined the rights and responsibilities of all members, regardless of their religious or tribal affiliations.

The Charter emphasized justice, mutual protection, and cooperation. It ensured that everyone in Medina, whether Muslim or non-Muslim, had a place in the community and was protected under its laws. This inclusive approach not only fostered peace but also created a resilient community that could withstand external threats and internal conflicts.

The Charter of Medina teaches us that resilience is not just an individual trait but a communal one. By fostering a supportive, inclusive environment, we can create communities that are strong, united, and capable of overcoming adversity.

The Prophet's Visits to the Sick

The Prophet Muhammad's practice of visiting the sick wasn't just a gesture of kindness; it was a vital component in weaving the social fabric of his community. By offering prayers, comfort, and companionship, the Prophet solidified the bonds that held his followers together. These visits were a testament to the power of compassion in fortifying social ties. They illustrate how simple, sincere acts of support can cultivate a resilient, interconnected society. In each visit, the Prophet demonstrated that even in times of personal hardship, maintaining strong, empathetic connections is key to building enduring resilience.

Leadership and Harmony

Prophet Muhammad's leadership was characterized by his ability to bring people together, foster mutual respect, and promote social harmony. His approach to leadership was not authoritarian; rather, it was collaborative and consultative. He listened to the opinions of his companions, valued their input, and often made decisions through consensus.

The Pledge of Aqabah

Before the migration to Medina, the Prophet Muhammad (PBUH) secured the Pledge of Aqabah, where representatives of the tribes of Aws and Khazraj from Medina committed to supporting the Prophet and his mission. This pledge was a key moment in building a supportive network that would provide the foundation for the Muslim community in Medina.

The Pledge of Aqabah demonstrates the importance of strategic alliances in building resilience. By securing the support of these influential tribes, the Prophet ensured that the Muslim community would have a strong, supportive network in their new home. This story underscores the value of building trust and cooperation among diverse groups to create resilient communities.

The Prophet's Relationship with the Companions

The Prophet Muhammad's relationship with his companions was one of mutual respect, love, and support. He would consult them on important matters, listen to their opinions, and treat them as equals. This relationship created a strong, supportive network that was essential for the resilience of the early Muslim community.

The Principle of Consultation: Shura as a Leadership Tool

Prophet Muhammad's approach to *shura* (consultation) with his companions was a cornerstone of his leadership style, exemplifying the balance between divine guidance and human wisdom. The practice of *shura* not only reflected the humility and inclusiveness of the Prophet's leadership but also laid the groundwork for a model of decision-making that is consultative, empowering, and future-oriented.

At the heart of the Prophet's leadership was his unwavering commitment to *shura*; an advisory system that involved seeking counsel from his companions on various matters, ranging from community governance to military strategy. This approach was not simply symbolic; it was a practical method of harnessing collective wisdom and ensuring that decisions were grounded in the realities of the time.

In the Quran, Allah emphasizes the value of consultation in governance, instructing the Prophet to consult with his companions: "And those who have responded to their lord and established prayer and whose affair is determined by consultation among themselves..." (Quran 42:38). This directive illustrates that even with divine guidance, the Prophet valued the perspectives and insights of those around him, recognizing the strength in diversity of thought.

Collective Wisdom Over Dictatorship: The Battle of Uhud

One of the most notable examples of *shura* was during the Battle of Uhud. The Prophet initially favored defending Medina from within the city's fortified walls. However, after consulting with a group of younger companions who preferred to confront the enemy outside the city, the Prophet respected their opinion and adjusted his plan accordingly, even though it did not align with his original instinct.

This event speaks volumes about his leadership style. It wasn't about imposing his will; rather, it was about fostering ownership and participation among the community. Even when the decision led to a challenging outcome, the Prophet never used it as an opportunity to undermine the process of consultation. He understood that the strength of the community lay in collective decision-making and shared responsibility.

Encouraging Debate and Diverse Perspectives: The Trench Strategy

During the Battle of the Trench, the Prophet once again demonstrated the importance of consultation. Faced with the threat of a massive coalition of enemy forces, Salman the Persian suggested an unconventional defensive strategy; digging a trench around Medina. This tactic was unfamiliar to the Arabs at the time but was widely used in Persia. Prophet Muhammad (PBUH) did not dismiss this new idea but embraced it after consulting with his companions.

This openness to innovative solutions, even when they came from outside the traditional framework, highlights the Prophet's adaptive leadership and ability to incorporate diverse perspectives. By leveraging the wisdom and experiences of his companions, the Prophet built a resilient, forward-thinking strategy that turned a potential defeat into a triumph.

Balancing Divine Guidance with Human Input: The Treaty of Hudaybiyyah

During the negotiations of the Treaty of Hudaybiyyah, the Prophet consulted his companions at various stages, particularly when the terms seemed unfavorable to the Muslim side. His ability to patiently listen to the concerns and grievances of his followers, while balancing this with his understanding of divine guidance, demonstrated the complexity and depth of *shura*.

The Prophet did not dictate decisions, but ensured that his companions were part of the decision-making process. Even though many felt disheartened by the concessions made in the treaty, Prophet Muhammad's consultation and patience paved the way for long-term peace and stability, proving that immediate setbacks could lead to greater future gains.

Empowering Others Through Consultation: The Delegation of Leadership

The Prophet also practiced *shura* by delegating responsibilities to capable individuals. His selection of leaders for different roles was based on their competencies, but consultation was a key part of this process. For instance, he appointed governors, military commanders, and judges who would consult with the community before making major decisions. This decentralization ensured that the Muslim community could function effectively and autonomously, even in the Prophet's absence.

Through *shura*, the Prophet empowered his companions to think critically, make informed decisions, and lead with confidence. This practice was vital for building an enduring leadership framework that could withstand the test of time.

A Model for Modern Leadership: Lessons from Shura

In today's world, *shura* provides a powerful model for leadership that is consultative, inclusive, and adaptive. The Prophet's approach shows that leaders should not view consultation as a sign of weakness but as a strategic strength. By involving others in decision-making, leaders can build trust, harness collective intelligence, and foster a culture of innovation and resilience.

Moreover, *shura* highlights the importance of listening to diverse perspectives and being open to new ideas. In an era of rapid change and complexity, the ability to adapt, learn from others, and incorporate different viewpoints is critical for success.

The Inclusion of Non-Muslims in the Medina Charter

Upon establishing the Muslim community in Medina, the Prophet Muhammad (PBUH) included various non-Muslim tribes in the Medina Charter, ensuring their rights and protection under Islamic governance. This act of inclusivity helped maintain peace and built a diverse, supportive network that contributed to the resilience of the entire community.

The inclusion of non-Muslims in the Medina Charter highlights the importance of inclusivity in building resilient communities. By ensuring that everyone in Medina, regardless of their religious background, was protected and had a place in the community, the Prophet created a supportive environment that could withstand internal and external threats.

The Prophet's Alliance with the Jewish Tribes of Medina

When Prophet Muhammad (PBUH) migrated to Medina, he didn't just establish a Muslim community; he forged alliances with the Jewish tribes through the Constitution of Medina. This was a strategic and groundbreaking move, not only creating peace and security but also showcasing the power of inclusive networks in fostering collective resilience. The pact wasn't just about coexistence; it was a model of mutual respect and shared responsibility. The Prophet understood that real resilience doesn't happen in isolation; it's built through alliances that transcend tribal, ethnic, or religious boundaries. This move laid the foundation for a resilient society capable of withstanding external threats while maintaining internal harmony. Source: *Al-Sirah al-Nabawiyyah*

The Prophet's Brotherhood Pact

In one of the most powerful examples of social resilience, the Prophet Muhammad (PBUH) established a brotherhood pact between the *Muhajirun* (immigrants from Mecca) and the *Ansar* (residents of Medina). Each *Ansar* family was paired with a *Muhajir* family, creating a network of mutual support and deep social integration. This wasn't merely charity; it was a strategic act of resilience-building. The pact turned two distinct communities into one united force, creating a social safety net that allowed the *Muhajirun* to not just survive but thrive in a new environment. It was a blueprint for turning vulnerability into strength through deliberate, supportive relationships. Source: *Fada'il al-A'mal*

The Prophet's Diplomatic Engagement with Non-Muslim Leaders

Prophet Muhammad (PBUH) wasn't just focused on building networks within his immediate community; he reached out globally, engaging with non-Muslim leaders through letters and diplomatic initiatives. He invited them to Islam, but more importantly, he sought peaceful relations. These efforts weren't just about expanding influence; they were about ensuring the resilience of the Muslim community on a global scale. By establishing diplomatic ties with rulers who didn't share his faith, the Prophet demonstrated that resilience isn't confined to internal strength. It's also about forging connections and building bridges, even with those who may seem like adversaries. This broader, inclusive vision of diplomacy added an external layer of protection and opportunity for growth. Source: *Dalail al-Khayrat*

The lessons from Prophet Muhammad's approach to community building are clear: strong social connections are essential for resilience. Whether through the Brotherhood of Muhajirun and Ansar, the Pledge of Aqabah, or the inclusive nature of the Medina Charter, the Prophet demonstrated that resilience is not an individual endeavor but a collective one. By fostering supportive, inclusive environments and building strong social networks, we can enhance our resilience and the resilience of our communities.

Key Takeaways:

- **Power of Community:** The secret gatherings at Dar al-Arqam highlight the importance of finding and nurturing a supportive community, especially when facing adversity. Social support provides strength, security, and a shared sense of purpose.

- **Compassionate Leadership:** The Prophet's regular visits to the sick show that small acts of kindness and support can strengthen social bonds, creating a network of care and resilience within the community.

- **Inclusive Networks:** The Prophet's alliance with the Jewish tribes in Medina underscores the importance of building inclusive networks that transcend differences. Collaboration with others, even those outside your immediate group, can provide mutual support and enhance resilience.

- **Mutual Support:** The brotherhood pact between the Muhajirun and the Ansar demonstrates that resilience is fostered through mutual support. Establish networks where members can rely on each other during difficult times, creating a foundation of collective strength.

- **Diplomatic Engagement:** The Prophet's engagement with non-Muslim leaders through letter writing shows that expanding your network to include diverse perspectives can strengthen resilience. Diplomatic and respectful communication is key to maintaining broad support systems.

- **Unity in Diversity:** The support the Prophet received from the Ansar in Medina demonstrates that strength comes from unity, even among diverse groups. Building bridges and fostering connections can create a resilient, cohesive community.

- **Consultation fosters collective ownership:** Engaging others in decision-making builds a sense of responsibility and ownership within the community.
- **Diversity strengthens decision-making:** The Prophet valued the input of companions from diverse backgrounds, showing that a wide range of perspectives leads to more robust and innovative solutions.
- **Openness to new ideas is critical:** The Prophet's willingness to adopt new strategies, like the trench during the battle, demonstrates the importance of being flexible and open to change.
- **Empowering others builds lasting resilience:** By consulting and delegating, the Prophet ensured that leadership was distributed, enabling the community to thrive even in his absence.

Reflection: Resilience is not built in isolation. Strengthen your social connections, engage in your community, and remember that a supportive network is a powerful source of resilience. Networks are the lifeblood of resilience. Build them inclusively, support them actively, and engage with them diplomatically to create a resilient foundation for any challenge.

In our own lives, we can apply these lessons by prioritizing our relationships, fostering mutual support, and building inclusive communities. By doing so, we can create a foundation of strength and resilience that will help us navigate life's challenges with confidence and grace.

3.3 Building and Maintaining Supportive Networks

In the journey toward resilience, the relationships we form and the environments we cultivate are not mere accessories; they are the bedrock upon which our strength is built. Drawing from the principles outlined in the life of Prophet Muhammad, we will explore how to build, maintain, and optimize the social networks and environments that are vital for personal and communal resilience.

Creating Meaningful Relationships

The Power of Intentional Connection: Creating deep, supportive connections begins with intentionality. Relationships that contribute to resilience aren't built overnight; they require effort, vulnerability, and a willingness to invest in others. It's essential to be selective about whom you let into your inner circle. Surrounding yourself with people who share your values, who challenge you to grow, and who offer unconditional support is crucial.

Start by identifying people in your life who embody the qualities you admire; integrity, empathy, and resilience; and seek to deepen those relationships. This can be done through regular communication, shared experiences, and offering support in times of need. Remember, the goal is not to have a large number of connections but rather to cultivate a few meaningful ones that provide mutual strength and encouragement.

Strategic Alliances

In the same way that Prophet Muhammad (PBUH) secured the Pledge of Aqabah to build a strong support network, you can develop strategic relationships that enhance your resilience. These alliances might be professional mentors, community leaders, or peers who offer wisdom, guidance, and support. Such relationships often require a reciprocal exchange of value; offering your skills, time, or resources in return for the support and guidance you receive.

By fostering these strategic alliances, you create a network of individuals who can provide counsel during difficult times and help you navigate challenges. These connections also broaden your perspective, exposing you to new ideas and strategies for overcoming adversity.

Nurturing Existing Bonds

Consistency and Care: Building relationships is just the beginning; maintaining and strengthening them requires consistent effort. Like any living organism, relationships need to be nurtured through regular attention and care. This involves not only spending time with those you care about but also being present and engaged when you do.

One effective strategy is to establish regular check-ins with key people in your life. This could be a weekly call with a close friend, a monthly coffee meeting with a mentor, or simply making a habit of sending thoughtful messages to loved ones. These small but consistent actions keep relationships strong and ensure that the bond deepens over time.

Conflict Resolution: No relationship is without its challenges, and how you navigate these difficulties is crucial to maintaining strong connections. The Prophet Muhammad's approach to resolving disputes; whether through patience, forgiveness, or seeking mutual understanding; offers valuable lessons.

When conflicts arise, address them with empathy and a willingness to listen. Seek to understand the other person's perspective and work towards a solution that honors both parties. Avoid letting misunderstandings fester, as unresolved issues can weaken the bond and erode trust over time. By handling conflicts with care and respect, you can strengthen your relationships and build a resilient network of support.

Optimizing Your Environment

Creating a Nurturing Space: Your physical and social environment plays a significant role in your ability to maintain resilience. An environment that nurtures growth and well-being is one that supports your physical, emotional, and mental health. Start by assessing your living space; does it promote relaxation, focus, and positivity? If not, consider making changes that align your surroundings with your goals for resilience.

This might involve decluttering your space to reduce stress, incorporating elements of nature to boost your mood, or creating designated areas for activities like meditation, exercise, or social gatherings. Your environment should reflect and reinforce your values, providing a sanctuary where you can recharge and grow.

Surrounding Yourself with Positivity: Just as Prophet Muhammad (PBUH) created a supportive community in Medina through the Charter, you can curate your social environment by surrounding yourself with positive influences. This doesn't mean avoiding challenges or difficult people entirely but rather seeking out individuals and communities that uplift and inspire you.

Identify the people, groups, and activities that contribute to your well-being and make a conscious effort to engage with them regularly. This might involve joining a community organization, participating in group activities, or simply spending more time with people who bring out the best in you. By intentionally surrounding yourself with positivity, you create an environment that fosters resilience and supports your personal growth.

3.4 Reflect and Apply

Personal Reflection

Evaluating Your Social Networks: Take a moment to reflect on your current social network. Are your relationships providing the support and encouragement you need to be resilient? Are there areas where your connections could be strengthened? Consider the quality of your relationships; do they bring you joy, challenge you to grow, and offer support in times of need?

Reflect on the balance of giving and receiving in your relationships. Are there connections where you feel you're giving more than you receive, or vice versa? Healthy relationships involve a mutual exchange of support, so it's important to assess whether your connections are balanced and fulfilling.

Assessing Your Environment: Next, evaluate your physical and social environment. Does your living space reflect your values and support your well-being? Are there elements of your environment that contribute to stress or negativity? Consider the people you spend the most time with; do they inspire you, challenge you, and support your growth?

Reflect on whether your environment and social connections are aligned with your goals for resilience. If not, think about what changes you can make to create a more supportive and nurturing environment.

Action Steps

Strengthening Social Connections

1. **Identify Key Relationships:** Make a list of the most important relationships in your life. Prioritize nurturing these connections by scheduling regular check-ins and spending quality time together.
2. **Reach Out and Reconnect:** If there are relationships that have weakened over time, take the initiative to reconnect. A simple message or a coffee invitation can reignite a meaningful connection.
3. **Join a Community:** Consider joining a group or organization that aligns with your interests and values. This could be a local club, a professional network, or a volunteer organization. Engaging with a community provides opportunities to build new connections and find support.

Optimizing Your Environment

1. **Declutter and Organize:** Start by decluttering your living space. Remove items that no longer serve you and organize your space to create a more peaceful and functional environment.

2. **Incorporate Positive Elements:** Add elements to your environment that uplift you; this could be plants, artwork, or inspirational quotes. Create spaces in your home that are dedicated to relaxation, creativity, and reflection.

3. **Surround Yourself with Positivity:** Seek out positive influences in your social environment. Spend more time with people who inspire you, and limit your exposure to negativity. Join groups or communities that align with your values and contribute to your growth.

By taking these steps, you can build and maintain supportive networks and create an environment that nurtures your resilience. Remember, resilience is not a solitary endeavor; it's strengthened through the connections we make and the environments we cultivate. By investing in your relationships and optimizing your surroundings, you lay the foundation for a resilient and fulfilling life.

CHAPTER GEM ELEMENTS

- ❖ **The Power of Trusted Support Systems**: Build and maintain strong, trusted relationships that provide emotional and practical support.

- ❖ **Community as a Source of Strength**: Engage with community networks to create a collective resilience that is greater than the sum of its parts.

- ❖ **Mutual Loyalty and Trust**: Foster relationships based on mutual loyalty and trust, which are essential for enduring support.

- ❖ **Unity in Diversity**: Leverage the strength that comes from diverse perspectives and backgrounds within a community.

- ❖ **Compassionate Leadership**: Lead with compassion, recognizing the importance of empathy and understanding in fostering resilience.

- ❖ **Proactively Seek Alliances**: Actively seek out and build alliances that can provide support during times of crisis.

- ❖ **Foster Mutual Respect in Networks**: Ensure that relationships within networks are built on mutual respect, which strengthens the bonds of support.

- ❖ **Inclusivity as a Strategic Strength**: Embrace inclusivity as a strategy for creating resilient networks that are adaptable and robust.

Chapter 4: Leading with Resilience

Organizational and Systemic Strength

In a world marked by rapid change and unpredictability, resilience is not just an individual trait; it's a vital organizational characteristic. The capacity for resilience within a system, be it an organization, a community, or a state, determines its ability to withstand crises, adapt to new challenges, and continue to thrive despite adversity. This chapter delves into the concept of organizational resilience, explores the systemic strengths that support it, and draws on the leadership of Prophet Muhammad (PBUH) to illustrate how resilient leadership can shape and sustain powerful, enduring institutions.

4.1 Resilience in Organizations

Why It Matters

Organizational resilience is the ability of an organization to anticipate, prepare for, respond to, and adapt to incremental change and sudden disruptions in order to survive and prosper. In today's complex, rapidly changing world, the importance of organizational resilience cannot be overstated. The challenges facing organizations; whether they be businesses, governments, or non-profits; are multifaceted and often unpredictable. Economic volatility, technological advancements, environmental crises, and global pandemics are just a few examples of the kinds of disruptions that can threaten the survival of even the most well-established entities.

Organizational resilience is not just about surviving these disruptions; it's about emerging from them stronger and more capable. A resilient organization can adapt to changes, recover quickly from setbacks, and continue to move forward with its mission. This resilience is anchored in the strength of its leadership and the robustness of its systems, complemented by the collective personal resilience of individuals. In this section, we'll delve into leadership and systems, as we've already thoroughly explored personal resilience in this book.

Systemic Strengths

The resilience of an organization is largely determined by the resilience of the systems that support it. These systems include the organization's culture, its processes and procedures, its technological infrastructure, and its human resources. A resilient system is one that is flexible, adaptable, and robust; capable of absorbing shocks and responding effectively to new challenges.

One key aspect of systemic resilience is redundancy. Just as ecosystems have multiple species that perform similar functions, resilient organizations have backup systems and processes that can take over when primary ones fail. This might involve having multiple suppliers, cross-training employees, or maintaining reserves of critical resources. Redundancy ensures that the organization can continue to function even when one part of the system is compromised.

Another critical factor is adaptability, remember, we covered that in earlier dimension!?, Resilient systems are not static; they evolve in response to new information and changing conditions. This requires a culture of continuous learning and improvement, where feedback is regularly gathered and used to make adjustments. Adaptable systems are also characterized by decentralized decision-making, allowing those closest to the problem to respond quickly and effectively.

4.2 The Prophet's Leadership in Action

Muhammad's approach to organizational resilience wasn't just about surviving adversity; it was about thriving through adaptability, delegation, and strategic planning. Let's dive into the following examples that clearly illustrate how he built a model of resilient leadership, proving his ability to structure and fortify a community under pressure.

Inclusive Leadership

The Black Stone story is a powerful example of organizational leadership and resilience in action. When the Kaaba was being rebuilt, a dispute arose among the tribes of Mecca about who would have the honor of placing the revered Black Stone back in its place. Tensions were high, and conflict seemed inevitable.

Prophet Muhammad, known for his wisdom even before prophethood, proposed a solution that displayed both leadership and a deep understanding of social harmony. He spread a cloth on the ground and placed the Black Stone in the center. He then invited all the tribal leaders to lift the cloth together, ensuring that everyone had an equal role. Once the stone was raised, he personally set it in its final position.

This solution not only resolved the conflict but also showed how inclusive leadership, creative problem-solving, and empathy can build resilience within a community. It was a lesson in fostering unity and navigating complex social dynamics, ensuring long-term stability and trust.

The Delegation of Responsibilities Among Companions

In any growing organization, the strain on leadership increases exponentially as responsibilities multiply. Prophet Muhammad's ability to recognize this challenge and address it by delegating key roles to capable leaders is a masterclass in organizational resilience. Rather than hoarding power or attempting to micromanage, he strategically distributed responsibilities across a team of trusted companions, thereby decentralizing authority without losing control of the vision.

By delegating essential roles to figures like Abu Bakr, Ali, and Khalid ibn al-Walid, Muhammad (PBUH) ensured that the Muslim community could function smoothly, even in his absence. Each of these leaders was assigned to an area where they excelled; Abu Bakr led prayer and governance, Ali handled judicial matters, and Khalid ibn al-Walid managed military strategy. This approach not only empowered the companions but also created a self-sustaining system of governance.

In modern organizational terms, this is the equivalent of building a leadership team that's both specialized and cross-functional, capable of operating independently but united under a shared mission. It's resilience through trust, empowerment, and foresight; traits that any organization looking to thrive under pressure should adopt. By decentralizing control, Muhammad (PBUH) created a robust, flexible structure, one that could absorb shocks and continue to function no matter the challenges faced.

The Formation of the Marketplace in Medina

A cornerstone of organizational resilience is the ability to create systems that can adapt to change and withstand external pressures. Upon settling in Medina, Prophet Muhammad (PBUH) recognized that the community needed an economic foundation that was both resilient and ethical. Instead of relying on the monopolistic marketplaces controlled by the Jewish tribes, he established a new, free, and regulated marketplace.

What's brilliant about this move is its dual nature: it wasn't just about setting up a market; it was about embedding ethical practices into the very fabric of the economy. The Prophet laid down guidelines to prevent exploitation and ensure fair competition, thus promoting an economic system where resilience wasn't just about surviving, but thriving on just principles.

This wasn't an ad-hoc decision. It was strategic. Muhammad (PBUH) understood that the lifeblood of any society is its economy, and a resilient economy needs to be both adaptable and fair. By fostering competition and setting ethical standards, he ensured the marketplace was stable enough to withstand economic fluctuations while remaining sustainable. In contemporary terms, this is akin to building an economic infrastructure that emphasizes transparency and fair practices, thereby safeguarding against both internal and external threats. It's a lesson in how robust systems are built on a foundation of values, not just efficiency.

Crisis Management

Another powerful aspect of Prophet Muhammad's leadership is his masterful approach to crisis management. Resilient leadership shines brightest in times of crisis, and the Prophet's ability to navigate through immense challenges was key to the survival and flourishing of the Muslim community. He didn't just focus on putting out immediate fires; he strategically laid the groundwork for long-term stability, ensuring that the community could endure future challenges.

Take, for example, the Constitution of Medina. This groundbreaking document wasn't just a short-term fix for tribal tensions; it established a framework for a cohesive, resilient community that could stand strong against internal divisions and external threats. By uniting the various tribes and faith groups under shared principles of justice and mutual protection, he preemptively diffused potential crises, securing peace and stability for the Muslim state.

Then there's the Battle of the Trench; a textbook example of adaptive strategy in the face of overwhelming odds. Faced with an alliance of tribes bent on annihilating the Muslim community, Muhammad (PBUH) didn't rely on conventional tactics. Instead, he embraced an innovative defensive strategy proposed by his companion Salman the Persian: digging a trench around the vulnerable parts of the city. This was an unfamiliar approach in Arab warfare, but it caught the enemy off guard and staved off defeat. This wasn't just resilience in action; it was strategic foresight and adaptability at their finest.

And even in historical stories predating his lifetime, like the Year of the Elephant, Muhammad (PBUH) drew profound lessons in resilience. The tale of Abraha's army, marching with elephants to destroy the Kaaba, and their miraculous defeat served as a recurring reminder to his community of divine protection. The Prophet used this event to instill a deep sense of faith and trust in Allah's plan, reinforcing that true resilience isn't only physical or strategic, but also rooted in spiritual conviction.

These examples show us that Muhammad's leadership was never just about reacting to immediate threats. It was about anticipating challenges, building robust structures, and crafting strategies that allowed the community to not just survive; but evolve and thrive. Whether it was through delegating responsibilities or establishing ethical economic systems, his model offers invaluable insights for building resilient organizations that can withstand and grow from adversity.

4.3 Building Organizational Resilience: Insights from the Prophet's Leadership

Drawing from the leadership of Prophet Muhammad, we find invaluable lessons in cultivating and sustaining resilience within organizations. Organizational resilience is not just about surviving in challenging times but thriving despite adversity. The essence of this resilience lies in the culture leaders cultivate, the systems they establish, and the foresight they apply to leadership.

Strategic Delegation Builds Sustainable Structures

By delegating responsibilities to capable leaders like Abu Bakr, Ali, and Khalid ibn al-Walid, Prophet Muhammad (PBUH) created a decentralized system that could function smoothly even in his absence. This teaches us that resilient organizations must empower individuals through trust and clear delegation, ensuring specialized leadership in critical areas.

Ethical Foundations Promote Economic Stability

By establishing an ethical and fair marketplace in Medina, the Prophet demonstrated that resilience isn't just about growth; it's about embedding values like fairness and justice into the core of the system. Sustainable economic resilience is built on ethical foundations, ensuring long-term stability.

Proactive Planning Creates Long-Term Resilience

Muhammad (PBUH) didn't just react to immediate problems; he anticipated future challenges by laying down systems (both in governance and economics) that could absorb shocks. Organizations that plan for long-term sustainability, rather than short-term fixes, are better equipped to weather crises.

Values-Based Leadership Drives Resilient Communities

The Prophet's decisions were rooted in ethical and moral principles, whether it was how he appointed leaders or structured the marketplace. Organizations that anchor their operations in strong values not only survive adversity but thrive through shared purpose and integrity.

Fostering a Resilient Culture

At the heart of any resilient organization is a culture that embraces change, promotes continuous learning, and encourages mutual support. Leaders play a pivotal role in shaping this culture. By modeling resilience; through their actions, decisions, and attitudes; they set the tone for the entire organization.

A resilient culture isn't built overnight; it requires consistent effort. Leaders must create environments where employees feel psychologically safe to express ideas, take risks, and learn from failures. This culture of safety fosters innovation and empowers employees to contribute actively to the organization's resilience. Encouraging continuous learning, whether through formal training or cross-functional collaboration, ensures that the organization is always adapting, always evolving.

In this environment, challenges are reframed as opportunities for growth. Successes are celebrated, and failures are seen as learning experiences. The goal is to create a workplace where collaboration is the norm, where every individual feels empowered to contribute to the organization's collective strength.

Implementing Redundant Systems

The Prophet's strategic defenses, such as the trench during the Battle of Trench, highlight the importance of redundancy in safeguarding communities. Similarly, organizations must implement systems that ensure continuity even when part of the system fails. This involves having backup plans; whether it's multiple suppliers, cross-trained employees, or reserves of essential resources.

Redundant systems create flexibility, enabling an organization to navigate unexpected challenges without being overly dependent on a single resource or process. It's about building in the capacity to absorb shocks, maintain operations, and continue serving your mission, no matter what obstacles arise.

Decentralizing Decision-Making

Decentralized decision-making is a cornerstone of resilient systems. By empowering individuals at all levels of the organization to make decisions, you enhance the organization's ability to respond quickly and effectively to challenges. This requires trust; a trust in your team's abilities and judgment, and a willingness to delegate authority.

Leaders should encourage autonomy and initiative among their employees. This doesn't mean a free-for-all, but rather, creating structures where teams can make decisions within clearly defined guidelines. A culture of collaboration is essential here, where solutions and ideas can emerge from any part of the organization, ensuring a dynamic and responsive approach to challenges.

Sustainable Leadership for Long-Term Resilience

Sustainable leadership is about more than guiding an organization through current challenges; it's about laying a foundation for future resilience. Leaders must recognize that their decisions today will impact the organization's ability to thrive in the long run.

Resilient leaders model the behaviors they wish to see; adaptability, transparency, and a commitment to continuous improvement. They prioritize the well-being of their employees, understanding that the health of the organization is closely tied to the well-being of its people. This includes promoting work-life balance, providing access to mental health resources, and fostering a supportive environment.

Moreover, sustainable leaders focus on long-term goals, making decisions that contribute to the organization's future success. They build diverse leadership teams, bringing a wide range of perspectives and approaches to the table, which is crucial for resilience. Finally, they invest in the next generation of leaders, ensuring that the organization will continue to thrive long after they're gone.

4.4 Reflect and Apply: Your Role in Building Organizational Resilience

Personal Reflection

Consider your role within your organization and ask yourself the following questions:

- How do you contribute to its resilience?
- Are you actively involved in fostering a culture of adaptability and continuous improvement?
- Are you prepared to take on a leadership role in a crisis?
- Reflect on how your actions, decisions, and attitudes impact the resilience of your organization. Think about your relationships with colleagues.

- Are you building strong, supportive connections that enhance collective resilience?
- Are you promoting open communication and collaboration?

Consider how you can play a more active role in creating a resilient culture.

Action Steps: Implementing Resilience-Building Practices

1. **Foster a Resilient Culture:** Start by promoting psychological safety and continuous learning within your team. Encourage open communication, adaptability, and build strong relationships with your colleagues.
2. **Prepare for Crises:** Advocate for the development and regular review of a crisis management plan in your organization. Participate in crisis drills and simulations, and ensure you understand your role in the event of a crisis.
3. **Model Sustainable Leadership:** If you're in a leadership position, lead by example. Demonstrate resilience, prioritize well-being, and maintain a focus on long-term goals. Build diverse teams and invest in the development of future leaders.
4. **Enhance Your Personal Resilience:** Work on your own adaptability and stress management skills. Engage in continuous learning, practice mindfulness, and build strong support networks both within and outside of work.

By taking these steps, you can contribute to building an organization that doesn't just survive but thrives in the face of adversity. Your role, whether as a leader or team member, is crucial in shaping the resilience of your organization. Embrace this responsibility and take proactive steps to ensure that your organization is prepared for whatever challenges the future may bring.

CHAPTER GEM ELEMENTS

- ❖ **Innovative Problem-Solving Under Pressure:** Cultivate the ability to think creatively and adapt quickly, especially in high-stress situations.
- ❖ **Learning from History:** Leverage historical insights to guide leadership decisions, using lessons from the past to shape the future.
- ❖ **Building Sustainable Systems:** Design systems and structures that ensure resilience and long-term sustainability, allowing organizations to thrive over time.
- ❖ **Strategic Empowerment:** Delegate responsibility effectively, fostering independent leadership and decentralized decision-making for increased agility.
- ❖ **Ethics as a Foundation:** Embed core values like fairness and justice into every facet of the organization to promote stability and trust.
- ❖ **Future-Proofing Through Planning:** Prepare for future challenges with forward-thinking strategies that ensure adaptability and crisis management.
- ❖ **Leading with Integrity:** Ground leadership in ethical principles, fostering a shared sense of purpose that strengthens the entire organization.
- ❖ **Creating a Culture of Growth:** Build an environment where innovation and learning are

constant, and employees feel empowered to take risks and learn from setbacks.

- ❖ **Flexible Backup Systems:** Implement redundancy to ensure continuity in the face of disruption, maintaining operational stability when things go wrong.
- ❖ **Distributed Decision-Making:** Empower teams at all levels to make informed decisions, creating a dynamic and responsive organization.
- ❖ **Sustainable Leadership:** Model resilience and adaptability, prioritizing the well-being of both the organization and its people for long-term success.

Chapter 5: Lifelong Learning

Growth Through Reflection and Education

In the journey of life, learning is not a destination but a continuous process that shapes who we are and how we respond to the world around us. This chapter explores the profound role that lifelong learning, rooted in reflection and education, plays in building resilience. By examining both modern perspectives on learning and the reflective practices of Prophet Muhammad, we uncover the essential elements that contribute to personal growth and resilience.

5.1 The Importance of Continuous Learning

Why Growth Mindset Matters in Resilience

A growth mindset; the belief that abilities and intelligence can be developed through effort and learning; is a cornerstone of resilience. When we adopt this mindset, challenges are not seen as insurmountable obstacles but as opportunities for growth. The concept of a growth mindset, popularized by psychologist Carol Dweck, underscores that our ability to learn and adapt is not fixed; it evolves with experience and reflection.

Resilience, at its core, is about adaptability as we previously discussed; but without learning, it is meaningless! Let me explain; the more we learn, the better equipped we are to navigate life's uncertainties. Embracing a growth mindset encourages us to continuously seek out new knowledge and skills, enabling us to overcome challenges and thrive in changing environments. This mindset transforms setbacks into learning experiences, fostering a sense of empowerment and agency in our lives.

The Science of Learning: Enhancing Cognitive Flexibility and Resilience

Modern neuroscience shows that learning and reflection have a profound impact on the brain's plasticity; the ability to reorganize itself by forming new neural connections. This cognitive flexibility is essential for resilience. When we engage in lifelong learning, we are not just acquiring new information; we are actively rewiring our brains to be more adaptable and capable of handling stress.

Reflection, a key component of learning, allows us to process experiences, draw insights, and apply those lessons to future situations. It is through reflection that we make sense of our experiences and integrate new knowledge into our existing frameworks. This ongoing process of learning and reflection strengthens our cognitive resilience, making us better equipped to face future challenges with creativity and confidence.

5.2 The Prophet's Reflective Practices

Prophet Muhammad's life offers profound examples of how reflection and continuous learning contribute to personal growth and resilience. His practices demonstrate the importance of solitude, thoughtful decision-making, and a deep commitment to learning.

Retreats to the Cave of Hira: Reflection and Solitude as Pathways to Growth

Before receiving the first revelation of the Qur'an, Prophet Muhammad (PBUH) would retreat to the Cave of Hira to engage in deep reflection and contemplation. These retreats were a form of spiritual and intellectual preparation, allowing him to connect with the divine and reflect on the moral and social issues of his time. This practice of solitude and reflection not only deepened his spiritual understanding but also prepared him for the monumental responsibility of prophethood.

The act of retreating to a quiet place for reflection is a powerful tool for personal growth. It allows us to step back from the noise of daily life, assess our experiences, and realign our goals with our values. In today's fast-paced world, finding time for solitude can be challenging, but it is essential for cultivating the clarity and inner strength needed to navigate life's complexities.

Thoughtful Decision-Making: Reflection as a Guide for Critical Decisions

Prophet Muhammad's decisions were deeply informed by reflection and consultation. One of the most striking examples of this is his approach to receiving and implementing the teachings of the Qur'an. The Prophet's engagement with the revelations was active and continuous; he reflected on the divine guidance, sought to understand its implications, and applied it to all aspects of life. His life-long learning from the Qur'an, as described in *Ash-Shifa (The Healing)*, illustrates how a commitment to reflection and education can enhance personal resilience.

Another profound example is the Night Journey and Ascension (Isra and Mi'raj). This extraordinary experience was not only a spiritual journey but also an educational one, filled with insights that guided the Prophet's leadership and strengthened his resolve. The journey symbolizes the pursuit of knowledge and the importance of seeking higher understanding, even in the face of overwhelming challenges.

Furthermore, the Prophet's encouragement of learning among his companions underscores his belief in the transformative power of education. As detailed in *Al-Sirah al-Nabawiyyah (The Prophetic Biography)*, he urged his companions to seek knowledge, whether through direct teaching or by learning from others. He understood that an informed and educated community is a resilient one, capable of facing challenges with wisdom and strength.

The Prophet's Deep Reflection on the Qur'anic Revelations.

Prophet Muhammad's relationship with the Qur'an went far beyond passive reception. He would immerse himself in deep contemplation, often spending long hours reflecting on the meanings of the verses revealed to him. He would even stand nearly the whole night in prayer, reciting a single verse of the Quran. Source: "Fada'il al-A'mal"

This was not just about absorbing knowledge; it was about truly internalizing it, understanding its broader implications, and then applying it to life. His habit of reflection wasn't just a ritual but a form of mental and spiritual training. It honed his capacity to navigate life's challenges, reinforcing his resilience and shaping him into a guide who not only taught others but also embodied the principles of lifelong learning.

The Prophet's Learning from the Rejection in Ta'if

The experience of Ta'if is often cited as one of the most painful moments in the Prophet's mission. In Taif, Prophet Muhammad went to call the people to Islam, but instead of welcoming him, the leaders rejected his message and incited the townspeople to violently drive him out. Despite being pelted with stones and severely injured, the Prophet responded with patience, praying for their guidance rather than seeking revenge. After being rejected and humiliated, he didn't sink into despair. Instead, he transformed the failure into a moment of profound learning. By reflecting on what went wrong and how he could refine his approach, he emerged with even greater clarity and purpose. Later, the Prophet approached the people of Medina with a strategic, patient approach, ensuring mutual commitment and understanding. This wasn't just resilience; it was the process of extracting lessons from adversity and continuously improving. The Prophet's ability to adapt and grow from setbacks shows the value of reflecting on experience, no matter how painful, and using it as fuel for future success. Source: "Al-Sirah al-Nabawiyyah"

The Prophet's Commitment to Literacy and Education

In the aftermath of the Battle of Badr, the Prophet Muhammad (PBUH) demonstrated his forward-thinking approach to education and resilience-building. Instead of punishment, he offered captured Quraysh their freedom in exchange for teaching literacy to ten Muslims. This decision reflects his deep understanding of the power of knowledge; not just for individuals but for society as a whole. By fostering education, the Prophet wasn't just teaching skills;

he was building the foundation for a resilient, informed community capable of facing future challenges with wisdom. This act illustrates his commitment to lifelong learning and its critical role in shaping a strong, enduring society. *Source: "Kitab al-Samarkandiyya"*

Each of these stories highlights the Prophet's continuous pursuit of learning and growth, using reflection, experience, and education to foster both personal and communal resilience.

Key Takeaways:

- **Continuous Reflection:** The Prophet's deep contemplation of Qur'anic revelations shows the value of continuous reflection as a means of growth. Lifelong learning is not just about acquiring knowledge but also about reflecting on and applying it.
- **Learning from Setbacks:** The Prophet's reflection on his experience in Ta'if teaches that setbacks are opportunities for learning and growth. Resilience is built by analyzing failures and using them to inform future actions.
- **Promoting Literacy:** The Prophet's emphasis on education and literacy after the Battle of Badr highlights the importance of knowledge in building a resilient community. Education empowers individuals and communities to face challenges with confidence and skill.

Reflection: Resilience is rooted in a commitment to lifelong learning. Reflect on your experiences, learn from setbacks, and continuously seek knowledge to grow stronger and more adaptable.

5.3 Cultivating Reflection and Learning: Enhancing Growth and Resilience

Lifelong learning and reflection are far more than abstract concepts; they are practical strategies that can significantly bolster personal growth and resilience. By integrating these practices into daily routines, you can cultivate a mindset of continuous improvement and adaptability. Here's how to put these principles into action.

Making Time for Reflection

Reflection serves as a crucial tool for personal development, enabling you to process experiences, extract insights, and drive continuous improvement. Here's how to weave reflection seamlessly into your daily life:

1. **Journaling:** Dedicate a few minutes each day to journaling. Use prompts like "What did I learn today?" or "What challenges did I encounter and how did I address them?" Journaling clarifies your thoughts, tracks progress, and reveals behavioral patterns that can be adjusted for growth.

2. **Meditation:** Incorporate meditation into your routine to cultivate mindfulness and self-awareness. Spend a few quiet moments each day focusing on your breath and observing your thoughts impartially. This practice helps you connect with your inner self,

understand emotional responses, and build resilience.

3. **Scheduled Reflection Time:** Allocate specific times for reflection, such as after work or before bedtime. This ensures that reflection becomes a regular practice rather than an occasional activity, fostering a consistent approach to personal growth.

Learning from Experience

Extracting lessons from experiences involves more than recalling events; it requires a structured approach to applying insights for future success. Consider these methods:

1. **Structured Debriefing:** After significant projects or challenges, conduct a debriefing session. Evaluate what succeeded, what could be improved, and the lessons learned. Engaging with colleagues or mentors during this process can provide diverse perspectives and enhance your understanding.

2. **Learning Logs:** Keep a learning log where you document experiences, insights, and lessons. Include context, actions taken, and outcomes. Reviewing this log regularly helps you track progress, identify patterns, and reinforce positive behaviors.

3. **Feedback Mechanisms:** Actively seek feedback to gain broader insights into your performance and behavior. Analyze feedback to identify areas for improvement and make necessary adjustments. Use

feedback as a catalyst for growth rather than criticism.

Commitment to Growth

A steadfast commitment to lifelong learning requires deliberate action and strategic planning. Here's how to sustain your growth:

1. **Setting Learning Goals:** Define clear, actionable learning goals. These goals might involve acquiring new skills, expanding knowledge, or improving personal attributes. Regularly review and adjust these goals to keep them challenging and relevant.
2. **Seeking Mentorship:** Connect with mentors who can provide guidance and support. Mentors offer valuable insights and help navigate challenges, accelerating your growth. Cultivate relationships with those who inspire and align with your learning objectives.
3. **Embracing Curiosity:** Maintain a curious mindset. Stay open to new ideas and experiences. Engage in diverse learning opportunities; read extensively, attend seminars, and participate in discussions that challenge your thinking and broaden your perspective.

5.4 Reflect and Apply: Personal Growth Through Lifelong Learning

Personal Reflection

Assess your current approach to learning and reflection. Consider:

How do you currently incorporate reflection into your routine? Evaluate the effectiveness of your methods and identify areas for enhancement.

What lessons have you recently learned from your experiences? Reflect on how these lessons have influenced your growth and how you can apply them moving forward.

Are you committed to lifelong learning? Examine your engagement with learning opportunities and your readiness to seek new knowledge and skills.

Action Steps: Implementing Lifelong Learning Practices

Adopt a Growth Mindset: Embrace challenges as opportunities for learning and development. Cultivate belief in your capacity to acquire new skills and knowledge through effort and perseverance.

Engage in Regular Reflection: Dedicate time to reflection through journaling, meditation, or quiet contemplation. Use these practices to process experiences and integrate new insights.

Pursue Continuous Learning: Prioritize lifelong learning by enrolling in courses, reading extensively, seeking mentorship, and remaining curious about the world. Learning should be a continuous journey, not confined to formal education.

Apply Lessons to Daily Life: Transform learning into practical applications. Whether enhancing decision-making, improving relationships, or advancing professional skills, apply your newfound knowledge to real-life situations.

Foster a Learning Culture: Inspire a culture of learning within your community or organization. Share your knowledge, support others in their learning journeys, and cultivate an environment where continuous improvement is valued.

By embracing lifelong learning and reflective practices, you can develop the resilience needed to navigate life's challenges and continue evolving. Let learning and reflection be guiding forces on your journey to personal and professional excellence.

CHAPTER GEM ELEMENTS

- ❖ **Continuous Engagement with Knowledge**: Commit to lifelong learning and the continuous acquisition of knowledge as a foundation for resilience.
- ❖ **Transformational Learning Experiences**: Seek out and embrace learning experiences that challenge and transform existing perspectives.
- ❖ **Encourage and Facilitate Learning in Others**: Promote a culture of learning and reflection within communities and organizations.

Chapter 6: Balance and Wellbeing

Nurturing the Whole Self

Resilience is often seen as the capacity to bounce back from adversity, but what truly underpins this ability is holistic well-being. Balance in life; across the physical, mental, emotional, and spiritual domains; is not a luxury but a necessity for resilience. When one aspect of well-being is neglected, it weakens the whole structure, making it harder to withstand life's inevitable challenges. In this chapter, we will delve into the life of the Prophet Muhammad (PBUH) to illustrate how his practices can guide us through this.

6.1 The Connection Between Well-being and Resilience

Why Balance is Crucial

Holistic well-being creates a strong foundation. Physical health ensures your body can endure stress and recover. Mental clarity allows you to think critically and make sound decisions. Emotional stability helps you maintain composure and empathy in trying times. Spiritual fulfillment offers a sense of purpose and connection that transcends momentary setbacks. Each of these elements feeds into the others, creating a cycle of strength that sustains resilience.

Body, Mind, Spirit

Balancing all aspects of well-being is essential for cultivating a resilient life. Imagine each facet; body, mind, and spirit; as a leg of a tripod. If one leg is weak or shorter than the others, the entire structure becomes unstable. Neglecting physical health, for example, can lead to mental fog and emotional distress, making it harder to stay grounded during challenges. Similarly, ignoring emotional needs can lead to burnout, even if the body and mind are in good condition.

Balance does not mean equal time and energy dedicated to each aspect at all times, but rather an awareness of when one area needs more attention. Physical exercise, mental stimulation, emotional connections, and spiritual practices all contribute to a well-rounded life. By nurturing each aspect, you build a reservoir of strength to draw from when faced with adversity.

6.2 The Prophet's Teachings on Balance

The Principle of Moderation

The teachings of Prophet Muhammad (PBUH) offer profound insights into the importance of balance and moderation in life. One of the key principles he emphasized was moderation in all things; be it in diet, worship, or daily routines. This moderation is not about limiting oneself but about creating a sustainable approach to living that honors all aspects of well-being.

The Prophet's Balanced Lifestyle

In the text *Al-Shamā'il al-Muhammadiyya*, the Prophet Muhammad (PBUH) is portrayed as someone who seamlessly integrated spiritual, physical, and social aspects of well-being into his life. He dedicated himself to prayer and fasting, yet he also ensured he took time for rest, family, and community. This balance was not a passive state but an active, conscious effort to maintain harmony in all areas of life.

For instance, despite his deep spiritual commitments, the Prophet would spend time with his family, engage with his community, and ensure he was well-rested. This balanced lifestyle is a testament to the idea that nurturing the whole self is not just about spiritual practices but about harmonizing every part of life.

The Story of the Three Men and Moderation

Another powerful illustration of the Prophet's emphasis on balance comes from the story of the three men who visited his household. After observing the Prophet's worship, they decided they would surpass him by fasting without break, praying all night, and avoiding marriage. The Prophet, upon hearing this, corrected them by emphasizing that while he fasted, he also ate; while he prayed, he also slept; and while he devoted himself to God, he also maintained his family life. This story, also from *Al-Shamā'il al-Muhammadiyya*, highlights that true devotion and well-being come from balance, not extremes.

The lesson here is clear: resilience is not about relentless striving without regard for the body's or mind's needs. It's about understanding that balance is what sustains us, allowing for long-term perseverance.

The Prophet's Approach to Food and Nutrition

The Prophet's approach to food, as described in *Al-Shamā'il al-Muhammadiyya*, also exemplifies his commitment to balance. He ate simple, wholesome foods like dates and barley, emphasizing moderation and mindfulness. He is well-known for promoting the idea that when eating, the stomach should be one-third for food, one-third for water, and one-third for air. This wasn't just about physical health; it was about nurturing the whole self. By being mindful of what he ate, he maintained a disciplined approach that nourished his body while also fostering spiritual awareness.

His diet was not about restriction but about choosing what was beneficial for both body and spirit. This approach teaches us that resilience is built not through indulgence or deprivation but through thoughtful moderation.

The Prophet's Regularity in Fasting

The Prophet Muhammad's approach to fasting was not only about spiritual devotion; it was an embodiment of holistic well-being. Beyond the obligatory Ramadan fasts, he engaged in regular voluntary fasting, creating a rhythm that balanced spiritual purification with physical health. His practice of fasting, interspersed with periods of mindful eating and hydration, serves as a powerful example of moderation. It wasn't about deprivation; it was about balance. This approach underscores how nurturing the body and soul in tandem is key to sustaining both resilience and inner peace. Source: "Dalail al-Khayrat"

The Prophet's Evening Routine

Prophet Muhammad's evening routine reveals a profound understanding of balance. His nights were spent in thoughtful prayer, meaningful family interaction, and deliberate rest. This routine wasn't simply about religious ritual or relaxation; it was a deliberate effort to nurture each facet of his being; spiritual, emotional, and physical. His resilience was rooted in this equilibrium. By ensuring that he gave time to both divine connection and personal well-being, he demonstrated that balance in daily life is essential for sustaining long-term strength and composure. Source: "Kitab al-Samarkandiyya"

The Prophet's Physical Activity

Prophet Muhammad (PBUH) actively engaged in physical activities like walking, horse riding, and participating in light sports. His physical activity wasn't merely incidental; it was a conscious part of his lifestyle. He understood that resilience isn't just a mental or spiritual practice; it's also about nurturing the body. Regular movement helped maintain his health and vitality, reinforcing the principle that physical well-being is foundational to overall balance. His lifestyle encourages a holistic approach to resilience, where nurturing the body is as vital as nurturing the mind and spirit. Source: "Fada'il al-A'mal"

These stories reflect the deeper truth that balance, in every aspect; whether spiritual, emotional, or physical; isn't just a byproduct of resilience; it is one of its core pillars.

Key Takeaways

1. **Holistic Well-being as the Foundation of Resilience**: True resilience comes from a balanced approach to life that nurtures the physical, mental, emotional, and spiritual aspects of self.

2. **The Importance of Moderation**: Excess in any area can lead to imbalance, weakening your overall resilience. Moderation, as taught by the Prophet Muhammad, creates sustainability in well-being.

3. **The Power of Balance in Daily Life**: Whether through diet, rest, or social interaction, maintaining balance across all life's domains is crucial for long-term growth and resilience.

4. **Mindful Practices Lead to Stronger Resilience**: Incorporating mindfulness in activities like eating and socializing strengthens the connection between body, mind, and spirit, fostering a more resilient self.

5. **Modeling a Balanced Life**: Following the example of the Prophet Muhammad, a balanced life is not just about spiritual fulfillment but about harmonizing every part of your life to build a resilient foundation.

6. **Physical Activity:** The Prophet's engagement in physical activities like walking and riding highlights the role of physical health in resilience. Maintaining physical fitness supports mental and emotional well-being, making you more resilient in all areas of life.

Reflection: Resilience requires a balanced approach to well-being. Prioritize moderation, maintain a holistic routine, and keep your body active to nurture your whole self and sustain long-term resilience.

By integrating these principles into your life, you can nurture your whole self, creating a resilient, balanced foundation capable of weathering life's challenges.

6.3: Creating Your Personal Well-being Plan

Self-Assessment: Understanding Your Needs

The first step toward crafting a robust well-being plan is a thorough self-assessment. Just as you would evaluate the health of a building by inspecting its foundation, walls, and roof, your well-being requires an honest appraisal of your physical, mental, and emotional states.

Physical Needs: Start by considering your physical health. Are you getting enough exercise? Is your diet balanced and nutritious? Do you sleep well and wake up refreshed? Physical health forms the bedrock of your overall well-being, providing the energy and vitality necessary to tackle life's challenges.

Mental Needs: Next, assess your mental health. Are your thoughts clear and focused, or do you often feel overwhelmed or distracted? Consider your cognitive habits; do you engage in activities that stimulate your mind, like reading or problem-solving? Mental well-being is crucial for resilience, enabling you to adapt and respond to life's unpredictability.

Emotional Needs: Finally, examine your emotional health. Do you feel emotionally balanced, or are there areas where you experience frequent stress, anxiety, or sadness? Emotional well-being is about understanding and managing your emotions, ensuring that you can maintain a stable and positive outlook even in difficult times.

By assessing these aspects of your life, you lay the groundwork for a well-being plan that addresses your unique needs.

Building a Routine: Practical Steps for Personalization

Once you've identified your needs, the next step is to build a routine that supports them. A well-constructed routine is like the scaffolding of a strong building; each piece reinforcing the other to create a stable structure.

Physical Routine: Start with your physical health. Incorporate regular exercise into your daily schedule; whether it's a morning jog, a yoga session, or strength training. Prioritize a balanced diet that nourishes your body without excess. Plan your meals ahead of time, focusing on whole foods, lean proteins, and plenty of vegetables. Ensure you get enough quality sleep each night, creating a bedtime routine that encourages relaxation, such as reading or meditating before bed.

Mental Routine: For mental well-being, allocate time for activities that challenge and engage your mind. This could be setting aside time each day for reading, learning a new skill, or engaging in creative hobbies. Practice mindfulness or meditation to help manage stress and improve concentration. Limit your exposure to negative news or social media, which can drain your mental energy, and instead focus on content that inspires and uplifts you.

Emotional Routine: To nurture your emotional health, build practices into your routine that help you process and regulate your emotions. Journaling can be an effective tool for reflecting on your feelings and experiences. Maintain social connections with friends and family, as these relationships provide emotional support and a sense of belonging. Engage in activities that bring you joy and relaxation, whether it's spending time in nature, listening to music, or pursuing a creative passion.

Sustaining Well-being: Consistency Amidst Chaos

The true test of a well-being plan is its durability during times of stress and upheaval. It's easy to maintain a routine when life is smooth, but resilience is built by sustaining your practices when challenges arise.

Adaptability: Build flexibility into your routine. Recognize that life's demands will shift, and your routine should be adaptable enough to accommodate these changes. If you can't fit in a full workout, a brief walk or stretching session can still keep you on track. If stress is high, even a few minutes of deep breathing or meditation can make a significant difference.

Accountability: Keep yourself accountable by setting specific goals and tracking your progress. Use tools like habit trackers, apps, or even a simple checklist to monitor your daily routines. Share your goals with a friend or mentor who can provide encouragement and support, helping you stay committed even when motivation wanes.

Reflection: Regularly revisit your self-assessment to ensure your routine continues to meet your needs. As your life evolves, so too should your well-being plan. Periodic reflection allows you to make necessary adjustments, ensuring that your routine remains aligned with your goals and circumstances.

6.4: Reflect and Apply

Personal Reflection: Assessing Your Current Practices

Take a moment to evaluate your current well-being practices. Are they comprehensive, addressing all aspects of your physical, mental, and emotional health? Do they provide you with the resilience needed to face daily challenges, or do you find yourself neglecting certain areas? This reflection is not about judgment but about understanding where you are and what steps are needed to enhance your well-being.

Action Steps: Integrating Holistic Well-being Into Daily Life

1. **Start Small:** Begin by incorporating small, manageable changes into your routine. Whether it's adding a 10-minute walk to your day, setting aside time for mindfulness, or making a healthier food choice, small steps can lead to significant improvements over time.
2. **Set Clear Goals:** Define specific, measurable goals for your well-being. Whether it's improving your sleep quality, increasing physical activity, or

reducing stress, clear goals provide direction and motivation.

3. **Monitor and Adjust:** Use tools like journals, apps, or checklists to monitor your progress. Regularly review your goals and adjust your routine as needed to ensure it continues to meet your evolving needs.

4. **Seek Support:** Don't hesitate to seek support from friends, family, or professionals. Whether it's a workout buddy, a counselor, or a mentor, having someone to share your journey with can make the process more enjoyable and sustainable.

5. **Embrace Flexibility:** Life is unpredictable, and rigidity can lead to burnout. Embrace flexibility in your routine, allowing for adjustments, when necessary, while maintaining a commitment to your overall well-being.

By following these steps, you can create a personalized well-being plan that nurtures all aspects of your life, helping you build resilience and thrive in the face of life's challenges.

CHAPTER GEM ELEMENTS

- ❖ **Holistic Well-Being:** Cultivate balance by integrating physical, mental, emotional, and spiritual health into everyday life through mindful practices that enhance overall resilience.

- ❖ **Moderation for Sustainability:** Practice moderation in all aspects, including diet, rest, and social interactions, to achieve a sustainable, balanced lifestyle that fosters long-term growth.

- ❖ **Mindful Practices for Resilience:** Incorporate mindfulness in daily activities, from nutrition to physical exercise, reinforcing the connection between body, mind, and spirit to build resilience.

- ❖ **Physical Activity for Strength:** Maintain regular physical exercise to support both mental and emotional well-being, ensuring a resilient foundation for life's challenges.

Chapter 7: Inner Strength

Spiritual and Moral Resilience

Spirituality and moral integrity aren't merely abstract ideas; they are potent sources of resilience, offering profound purpose and inner strength. During crises, when external supports may waver, it is often these spiritual and ethical foundations that sustain individuals, providing a beacon of light through the darkest times. In this chapter, we will delve into the life of the Prophet Muhammad (PBUH) to illustrate how his practices can guide us in nurturing these essential aspects of well-being to enhance resilience.

7.1 The Power of Spirituality and Ethics

Why Spirituality Matters

Spirituality connects us to something greater than ourselves, whether it be a higher power, the universe, or a deep-seated belief in a moral code. This connection fosters a sense of purpose, helping us understand our place in the world and our role within it. It offers a refuge during trials, providing the strength to endure and the perspective to see beyond immediate hardships.

Moral integrity, on the other hand, grounds us in principles that dictate how we interact with the world. When faced with challenges, individuals who adhere to a strong ethical code are less likely to compromise their values, even under pressure. This steadfastness contributes to resilience, as it allows for consistent behavior that is aligned with one's beliefs, fostering a sense of coherence and self-respect.

The Science of Spirituality

Research increasingly supports the idea that spiritual practices and ethical values play a significant role in enhancing psychological resilience. Studies have shown that individuals who engage in regular spiritual practices, such as prayer or meditation, often experience lower levels of stress and anxiety. These practices encourage mindfulness and a focus on the present moment, which can reduce the impact of negative emotions and foster a sense of calm and control.

Moreover, ethical behavior has been linked to higher levels of well-being and life satisfaction. When people live according to their values, they experience greater self-esteem and a stronger sense of purpose, both of which are critical components of resilience. The consistency and predictability that come with living an ethically driven life also help in building trust and support within communities, further reinforcing resilience.

7.2 The Prophet's Ethical and Spiritual Resilience

Belief in Faith and Destiny (Tawakkul and Qadr)

Early Prophethood Challenges

Prophet Muhammad's life offers profound examples of how unwavering faith and moral integrity can serve as pillars of resilience. It is based on core principles; which are called in Islamic teachings, Tawakkul (trust in God's plan) and Qadr (belief in destiny). They instill a sense of peace and acceptance, even in the face of hardship. This principle encourages individuals to be comfortable with discomfort, understanding that everything that happens is part of a divine plan.

Tawakkul and Qadr emphasize acceptance and trust in the face of uncertainty, which is a core aspect of resilience. This principle teaches that while one must strive and exert effort, the outcome is ultimately beyond human control, fostering a mindset that is prepared for and accepting of all possibilities. This aligns with modern psychological practices that encourage acceptance and mindfulness as tools for coping with adversity.

Curiously, if you have Muslim friends, you might notice them frequently saying "Alhamdulillah" in various situations. This word embodies the above concept.

Let me elaborate; in Islam, the phrase *Alhamdulillah* carries a profound meaning beyond mere gratitude; it embodies an acceptance of life's unfolding as part of a larger, divine plan. Muslims say *Alhamdulillah* not only when things go well but also when they face hardship, recognizing that both joy and struggle are part of a greater, purposeful design. It's not about being content just because life is smooth, but about finding solace in the belief that everything, whether seemingly good or bad, is written with wisdom and mercy.

The phrase translates to "praise be to Allah" and serves as a constant reminder that every moment; whether a success or a challenge; is an opportunity to reflect on the blessings that often go unnoticed. When a Muslim says *Alhamdulillah*, they are not just expressing gratitude for the obvious joys in life but are also acknowledging the subtle blessings that hardship can bring. It's an active surrender, a way of saying, "I may not understand it, but I trust in the higher order behind it."

This mindset encourages resilience because it shifts focus from the external circumstance to an inner peace, a recognition that things unfold according to a plan greater than oneself. *Alhamdulillah* becomes a mantra of strength; whether in moments of joy or sorrow, it is an expression of unshakable trust in a divine narrative that is always in motion.

Back to Muhammad; from the earliest days of his prophethood, he faced intense persecution and adversity. Despite the constant threats to his life and the rejection of his message, he remained steadfast in his mission, driven by a deep sense of spiritual purpose and moral responsibility.

One of the most striking examples of the Prophet's spiritual resilience is his experience in Ta'if. After being rejected and physically assaulted by the people of Ta'if, the Prophet could have easily succumbed to despair. Instead, he turned to prayer, expressing his vulnerability to God but reaffirming his trust in divine mercy. This prayer, uttered in a moment of profound weakness, exemplifies the inner strength derived from a deep spiritual connection. It was this unshakeable faith that allowed him to persevere in the face of overwhelming opposition, demonstrating that true resilience is often born from spiritual endurance.

Living by Values

The Prophet's life was a testament to the power of living by strong ethical principles. His resilience was not just a result of spiritual fortitude but also of his unwavering commitment to moral values. This is evident in how he led both in times of peace and conflict, always adhering to principles of justice, compassion, and forgiveness.

One of the most significant instances of his moral resilience was during the Conquest of Mecca. After years of persecution, the Prophet entered Mecca as a victorious leader. In such a moment, many would have sought revenge against their former oppressors. However, the Prophet chose a path of forgiveness, declaring a general amnesty for those who had wronged him and his followers. This act of mercy, despite having the power to exact retribution, highlighted his profound inner strength and commitment to ethical values. It set a moral standard that transcended personal grievances, showing that true resilience is not just about enduring hardship but also about maintaining integrity and compassion in the aftermath.

Another powerful example is the Night of Badr. On the eve of the Battle of Badr, facing a far larger and better-equipped enemy, the Prophet spent the night in deep prayer, seeking divine support. This act of spiritual resilience underscored the importance of reliance on higher principles and guidance in moments of uncertainty. The victory that followed was not just a military success but a testament to the power of faith and moral steadfastness.

I know, hungry for more? let me enlighten you with more stories.

The Prophet's Night Prayers (Tahajjud)

Even after the obligatory five daily prayers were established, Prophet Muhammad (PBUH) continued to perform the night prayers, Tahajjud. This was not merely an act of worship; it was a powerful source of spiritual strength and resilience. In the stillness of the night, he would seek solace and guidance, a personal refuge during the most difficult times of his life. These prayers provided him with an anchor; a connection to something greater than the immediate struggles he faced. Tahajjud was where inner strength was fortified, where spiritual endurance was cultivated. It wasn't just about praying; it was about aligning with a purpose that transcended the trials of the world, allowing him to face even the harshest challenges with calm and resolve. Source: "Dalail al-Khayrat"

The Prophet's Reaction to the Slaughter of His Companions at Bir Ma'una

When the news came that seventy of his closest companions had been brutally slaughtered at Bir Ma'una, the Prophet Muhammad (PBUH) was deeply grieved. This wasn't just a communal tragedy; it was personal, a devastating blow. But rather than succumb to despair, he responded with an unshakable patience. He prayed for the souls of the martyrs and continued forward, steadfast in his mission. His spiritual resilience allowed him to transcend the overwhelming grief, focusing not on revenge but on the greater purpose ahead. This reaction showed the strength that comes from an unwavering connection to a higher cause, a mission too vital to be derailed by personal loss. Source: "Al-Sirah al-Nabawiyyah"

The Prophet's Forgiveness of Hind and Wahshi

In one of the most powerful acts of moral resilience, Prophet Muhammad (PBUH) forgave Hind bint Utbah and Wahshi, two individuals directly responsible for the brutal killing of his beloved uncle, Hamza. After the conquest of Mecca, he had every right to demand retribution, but instead, he chose forgiveness. This act wasn't just about mercy; it was about embodying a higher moral principle. His ability to forgive those who had inflicted such deep personal pain speaks to an inner strength rooted in compassion and mercy, demonstrating how resilience is not just about enduring pain, but about rising above it and choosing the path of moral clarity. Source: "Kitab al-Samarkandiyya"

Key Takeaways

1. **Spirituality and Moral Integrity as Pillars of Resilience:** Spirituality provides a sense of purpose, and moral integrity offers consistency in behavior, both of which are crucial for enduring and overcoming life's challenges. The Prophet's experiences, such as his prayer in Ta'if, demonstrate how deep spiritual faith can sustain one through the most trying times, offering a model of resilience based on inner strength and divine trust. The true resilience involves not just adapting to what happens but also trusting that there's a higher wisdom behind every event can deepen this model's spiritual dimension.

2. **The Science of Spirituality and Resilience:** Research supports the idea that spiritual practices reduce stress and anxiety, while ethical living enhances well-being and life satisfaction, contributing to greater psychological resilience.

3. **Moral Resilience in Action:** The Prophet's choice to forgive during the Conquest of Mecca and

his reliance on prayer before the Battle of Badr illustrate how living by ethical principles strengthens resilience, enabling one to maintain integrity and compassion even in the face of adversity.

4. **Spiritual Discipline:** The Prophet's commitment to night prayers (Tahajjud) exemplifies the role of spiritual discipline in building inner strength. Regular spiritual practice provides the foundation for resilience in the face of life's challenges.

5. **Patience in Grief:** The Prophet's response to the loss of his companions at Bir Ma'una shows the power of patience and trust in divine wisdom. Spiritual resilience involves accepting loss with grace and maintaining faith in the face of adversity.

6. **Forgiveness as Strength:** The Prophet's forgiveness of those who wronged him, like Hind and Wahshi, demonstrates the moral resilience that comes from mercy. True strength lies in the ability to forgive and let go of grievances, freeing oneself from the burden of hatred.

7. **Ethical Decision-Making**: By valuing consultation, the Prophet Muhammad (PBUH) exemplified a form of moral resilience that prioritizes justice, respect for different perspectives, and inclusivity in decision-making processes.

Reflection: Inner strength is rooted in spiritual and moral resilience. Cultivate spiritual discipline, practice patience in adversity, and embrace forgiveness as a path to true strength and inner peace.

By integrating spirituality and moral integrity into our lives, we can cultivate a deep reservoir of inner strength that not only helps us navigate personal trials but also elevates our interactions with others, fostering a more resilient and compassionate society.

7.3: Building Spiritual and Moral Strength

Strengthening Faith

Cultivating spiritual resilience requires an intentional effort to deepen one's faith and connection to a higher purpose. This connection can be a powerful source of inner strength, providing stability and clarity during difficult times. Here are some strategies to strengthen your faith:

- **Prayer**: Prayer is one of the most profound ways to nurture spiritual resilience. It creates a direct line of communication with the divine, offering a sense of peace, guidance, and reassurance. Regular prayer, especially during moments of uncertainty or stress, can anchor your spirit, allowing you to draw on a source of strength that transcends the immediate challenges.

- **Meditation**: Meditation, a practice of focused attention and mindfulness, allows you to cultivate a deeper connection with your inner self and the divine. By setting aside time each day to meditate, you can develop a sense of inner calm and clarity, which are essential for resilience. Meditation also encourages reflection, helping you to process experiences and align your actions with your spiritual goals.

- **Connecting with a Higher Purpose**: Understanding and embracing your higher purpose is fundamental to spiritual resilience. This might involve dedicating yourself to a cause greater than yourself, whether it's serving your community, pursuing justice, or simply striving to live a life of kindness and integrity. When your actions are guided by a higher purpose, you can find the strength to persevere through challenges, knowing that your efforts contribute to something meaningful.

Living with Integrity

Moral resilience is built on the foundation of living in accordance with your values. When your actions consistently align with your ethical principles, you create a strong sense of self-respect and inner harmony, both of which are crucial for enduring difficult times.

- **Aligning Actions with Values**: To develop moral resilience, it's essential to live authentically by ensuring that your daily actions reflect your core values. This means making decisions that are consistent with what you believe is right, even when it's difficult or unpopular. By doing so, you reinforce your moral compass, making it easier to navigate ethical dilemmas and maintain your integrity in the face of adversity.

- **Practicing Honesty**: Honesty is a key component of moral resilience. Being truthful in your words and actions not only fosters trust and credibility but also strengthens your inner resolve. When you practice honesty, you avoid the internal conflict that comes with deceit or compromise, allowing you to face challenges with a clear conscience and a strong sense of self-worth.

Spiritual Practices for Resilience

Incorporating spiritual practices into your daily routine can significantly enhance your resilience by fostering a deeper sense of inner peace and connection to others.

- **Gratitude**: Practicing gratitude involves regularly reflecting on the blessings in your life, no matter how small. This practice shifts your focus from what is lacking to what is abundant, cultivating a positive mindset that is essential for resilience. Gratitude helps you to appreciate the present moment, reduces stress, and fosters a sense of contentment that can carry you through tough times.
- **Mindfulness**: Mindfulness is the practice of being fully present in the moment, without judgment. By paying attention to your thoughts, feelings, and surroundings, you can develop a greater awareness of your inner state and respond to challenges with calmness and clarity. Mindfulness helps you to manage stress, reduce anxiety, and maintain emotional balance, all of which contribute to resilience.

- **Community Service**: Engaging in community service allows you to connect with others and contribute to the well-being of your community. Serving others not only strengthens your sense of purpose but also fosters empathy and compassion, which are essential for building moral and spiritual resilience. Through community service, you develop a broader perspective, recognizing that your struggles are part of the shared human experience, and this connection can provide strength and support.

7.4: Reflect and Apply

Personal Reflection

Reflection is a crucial step in building spiritual and moral resilience. It involves taking the time to assess your beliefs, values, and actions, ensuring that they are aligned with your highest principles. Consider the following questions as you reflect:

- **What are my core spiritual beliefs?** Reflect on the beliefs that guide your life. How do these beliefs influence your decisions and actions? Are there areas where your faith could be deepened or clarified?
- **Do my actions reflect my values?** Evaluate how consistently your actions align with your ethical principles. Are there situations where you've compromised your values? How can you strengthen your commitment to living with integrity?

- **How do I respond to challenges?** Consider how you react to difficult situations. Do you rely on your spiritual practices and moral compass to guide you, or do you struggle to maintain your inner strength? How can you better prepare yourself to respond resiliently in the future?

Action Steps

To integrate spiritual and moral resilience into your daily life, consider the following practical steps:

- **Establish a Daily Prayer or Meditation Routine**: Dedicate time each day to connect with your spiritual beliefs through prayer or meditation. This practice will help you cultivate inner peace and strengthen your resilience.
- **Live Your Values**: Make a conscious effort to align your actions with your values. Whether in personal relationships, work, or community involvement, strive to be consistent in living out your ethical principles.
- **Practice Gratitude and Mindfulness**: Incorporate gratitude and mindfulness into your daily routine. Start or end your day by reflecting on what you are grateful for, and practice mindfulness throughout the day to stay grounded and present.
- **Engage in Community Service**: Look for opportunities to serve others in your community. This can be as simple as volunteering your time or offering support to those in need. Community

service reinforces your sense of purpose and connects you to a larger community of resilience.

By committing to these practices, you can build a strong foundation of spiritual and moral resilience, enabling you to navigate life's challenges with grace and integrity. This inner strength will not only sustain you in difficult times but also enrich your daily life, guiding you toward a path of purpose, fulfillment, and growth.

CHAPTER GEM ELEMENTS

- ❖ **Spiritual and Moral Foundations for Resilience:** Spirituality provides purpose, while moral integrity fosters consistency and well-being. Together, they reduce stress, enhance life satisfaction, and form a resilient foundation that helps navigate life's challenges with strength and grace.

- ❖ **Resilience Through Forgiveness:** Practicing forgiveness, even in the face of great wrongs, demonstrates moral strength. Letting go of grievances frees one from the weight of anger and fosters personal growth.

- ❖ **Spiritual Discipline for Inner Strength:** Regular spiritual practices, such as prayer and reflection, cultivate inner strength, preparing individuals to face adversity with a calm and steady heart.

- ❖ **Patience and Trust in Divine Wisdom:** Accepting loss and setbacks with patience, while maintaining faith in a higher wisdom, strengthens one's ability to endure hardships with resilience.

- ❖ **Ethical Decision-Making and Inclusivity:** Moral resilience also involves seeking justice and inclusivity in decision-making, valuing diverse perspectives, and upholding ethical principles.

Chapter 8: Strengthening the Body

The Role of Physical Health

In this chapter, we'll first explore the biological foundations of resilience, shedding light on how our bodies contribute to our capacity to endure and thrive. We'll then look at the Prophet's practical advice and personal example, demonstrating how his focus on health laid the groundwork for physical resilience. And finally, we'll walk through practical steps on how to assess and enhance your own physical health, building a body that supports not just survival, but thriving in the face of adversity.

By the end, you'll see how physical resilience isn't just a nice-to-have; it's a fundamental part of becoming the best, most resilient version of yourself. You'll understand why neglecting your body can undermine your ability to navigate life's challenges and how prioritizing your health is essential for long-term success.

8.1 Biological Foundations of Resilience

The Science of Resilience

Resilience is not just a psychological trait; it has deep roots in our biology. Our physical health and brain chemistry play critical roles in determining how we respond to stress and adversity. The body's ability to recover from setbacks is influenced by factors such as immune system strength, hormonal balance, and neurotransmitter activity.

For instance, a well-functioning body can produce and regulate hormones like cortisol and adrenaline, which are essential in managing stress. When these systems are balanced, we are more likely to remain calm and composed in the face of challenges, thereby enhancing our resilience.

Furthermore, genetic factors also contribute to our baseline resilience. Some individuals may inherit a natural predisposition to handle stress more effectively, thanks to variations in genes related to neurotransmitter production and stress hormone regulation. However, these genetic factors are not fixed destinies but can be influenced by our environment and lifestyle choices, which brings us to the next crucial point.

Epigenetics and Lifestyle

Epigenetics, the study of how behaviors and environment can cause changes in gene expression, reveals that our lifestyle choices can significantly impact our resilience. While we may have genetic predispositions, the way we live our lives; our diet, exercise routines, sleep patterns, and stress management techniques; can modify how our genes express themselves.

For example, regular physical activity has been shown to enhance the expression of genes associated with positive stress responses, while a sedentary lifestyle can do the opposite. Similarly, a balanced diet rich in nutrients supports brain health and can influence the production of neurotransmitters that regulate mood and stress responses. This means that by making mindful lifestyle choices, we can actively enhance our biological resilience, potentially offsetting genetic vulnerabilities and strengthening our capacity to handle life's challenges.

8.2 The Prophet's Emphasis on Health

Healthy Living Principles

Prophet Muhammad (PBUH) placed a strong emphasis on physical health, understanding its integral role in overall well-being and resilience. His teachings on diet, exercise, and hygiene are timeless principles that promote a balanced and healthy life. He advocated for moderation in eating, recognizing the importance of not overindulging while ensuring the body received adequate nourishment. His recommendation of fasting, for example, not only served spiritual purposes but also contributed to physical health by allowing the body to cleanse and regenerate.

Exercise was another crucial component of the Prophet's approach to health. He encouraged his followers to engage in physical activities such as walking, riding, and swimming, emphasizing that a strong body supports a strong mind and spirit. Additionally, the Prophet stressed the importance of cleanliness and hygiene, understanding that a clean and well-maintained body is less prone to illness and better equipped to handle the demands of life.

Physical Resilience

The Prophet's attention to health was not merely about avoiding illness; it was about building a body capable of enduring hardship and contributing to one's overall resilience. His life provides several examples of how physical health underpinned his resilience.

The Prophet's Participation in Physical Activities

The Prophet Muhammad (PBUH) actively participated in physical activities such as wrestling, horse riding, and archery. These were not just recreational activities but also ways to maintain physical health and readiness. His involvement in these activities highlighted the importance of physical strength as a component of overall resilience. By staying physically active, the Prophet ensured that he was prepared to face both the physical and mental challenges of leadership and daily life.

One well-known story involves the Prophet Muhammad engaging in friendly competition with his wife Aisha, including racing with her. They raced twice; Aisha won the first race, and later, after she had gained some weight, the Prophet won the second race. This playful and lighthearted interaction reflects the Prophet's loving and kind relationship with his wives, demonstrating that he valued joy and companionship in marriage.

The Prophet's Recommendations for Physical Health

The Prophet Muhammad (PBUH) offered practical advice on maintaining health, which included the benefits of fasting, moderation in eating, and cleanliness. He advised eating in moderation, leaving a third of the stomach for food, a third for water, and a third for air, promoting a balanced approach to nourishment. His teachings on cleanliness; emphasizing the importance of regular washing and keeping the body pure; were not just about ritual purity but also about maintaining a healthy body. These practices, grounded in both spiritual and physical wisdom, contribute to the overall resilience of an individual by ensuring the body is strong, healthy, and capable of withstanding the pressures of life.

The Prophet's Dietary Practices

The Prophet Muhammad's approach to food wasn't just about sustenance; it was a deliberate strategy for maintaining physical and mental resilience. He advocated for a diet rich in wholesome, nutrient-dense foods like dates, honey, and olive oil; ingredients we now recognize as nutritional powerhouses. But what's more important is how he emphasized moderation in eating, a balance that kept his body strong without excess. His dietary habits weren't just personal; they were a blueprint for his followers, demonstrating how mindful consumption builds not only physical strength but also mental clarity and endurance. This practice is a timeless reminder that resilience isn't just about surviving hard times; it's about how we fuel ourselves to thrive through them. *Source: "Fada'il al-A'mal"*

The Prophet's Participation in the Digging of the Trench

Leadership isn't about sitting on the sidelines, and the Prophet Muhammad (PBUH) embodied this truth during the Battle of the Trench. Despite his position as a leader, he was shoulder-to-shoulder with his companions, physically digging the trench to defend their community. This wasn't just a symbolic gesture; it was an act of physical resilience that demonstrated the importance of maintaining strength and endurance, no matter your role. His participation wasn't just inspiring; it sent a clear message that physical effort is integral to leadership and survival. In a world that often elevates intellect over the body, the Prophet's actions remind us that true resilience is grounded in the physical, that enduring hardship requires not just mental toughness but physical capability. *Source: "Al-Sirah al-Nabawiyyah"*

The Prophet's Practice of Siwak (Teeth Cleaning)

Even in the smallest acts, the Prophet Muhammad (PBUH) showed the significance of physical well-being. His regular use of the *siwak*; a natural toothbrush; wasn't just about cleanliness, it was an essential practice of health and hygiene. In Islam, physical cleanliness is deeply connected to spiritual purity, and the Prophet's attention to oral hygiene reflected this holistic view. By prioritizing this simple but powerful act of self-care, he emphasized that resilience isn't just about enduring life's big challenges but also about caring for the body in daily routines. This attention to detail, this prioritization of health even in minor aspects, forms the backbone of a resilient, healthy life. *Source: "Kitab al-Samarkandiyya"*

Key Takeaways

1. **Biological and Genetic Foundations**: Our resilience is deeply rooted in our biology, with physical health and brain chemistry playing pivotal roles. While genetics influence our baseline resilience, lifestyle choices such as diet, exercise, and sleep can significantly modify gene expression, enhancing our capacity to handle stress.

2. **Prophet Muhammad's Emphasis on Health**: The Prophet's teachings on health; covering diet, exercise, and hygiene; highlight the importance of maintaining a strong and healthy body as part of overall resilience. His practices demonstrate that physical health is not only about avoiding illness but also about building a body capable of enduring and thriving in the face of adversity.

3. **Healthy Habits:** The Prophet's dietary practices, including his preference for wholesome foods, emphasize the importance of maintaining healthy habits. Physical health is foundational to overall resilience, supporting both mental and emotional well-being.

4. **Active Participation:** The Prophet's participation in physically demanding tasks, like digging the trench during the Battle of the Trench, shows the importance of physical strength and endurance. Staying physically active ensures that you are prepared to face challenges head-on.

5. **Regular Hygiene:** The Prophet's practice of using the siwak for oral hygiene highlights the importance

of cleanliness and self-care. Regular attention to physical health, including hygiene, contributes to overall well-being and resilience.

Reflection: Physical health is a cornerstone of resilience. Establish healthy habits, stay active, and prioritize self-care to strengthen your body and support your resilience in all areas of life.

8.3 Developing Physical Resilience

Building physical resilience is essential for overall well-being and plays a crucial role in enhancing mental and emotional strength. A resilient body supports a resilient mind, and the two are inextricably linked. In this section, we will explore how to assess and improve your physical health, offering practical strategies to build a resilient body and discussing the powerful connection between physical and mental resilience.

Health Assessment: Evaluating Your Physical Health

The first step in developing physical resilience is a comprehensive assessment of your current health. This involves examining key areas such as diet, exercise, sleep, and stress management.

1. **Diet**: Reflect on the quality of your diet. Are you consuming a balanced intake of nutrients, or do you rely heavily on processed foods? Consider the variety in your diet, the portion sizes, and how often you eat. A healthy diet rich in fruits, vegetables, lean proteins, and whole grains is foundational for

physical resilience. It provides the energy and nutrients necessary for the body to function optimally, recover from stress, and maintain overall health.

2. **Exercise**: Assess your physical activity levels. Are you engaging in regular exercise that includes cardiovascular, strength, and flexibility training? The American Heart Association recommends at least 150 minutes of moderate aerobic activity or 75 minutes of vigorous activity per week, along with muscle-strengthening activities on two or more days a week. Regular exercise strengthens the cardiovascular system, improves muscle tone, enhances flexibility, and boosts overall endurance, all of which contribute to physical resilience.

3. **Sleep**: Evaluate your sleep patterns. Are you getting enough quality sleep each night? Poor sleep can significantly impair physical and mental resilience, leading to decreased immune function, impaired cognitive performance, and heightened stress responses. Good sleep hygiene, including a consistent bedtime routine and a sleep-conducive environment, is crucial for restorative sleep.

4. **Stress Management**: Consider how you manage stress. Chronic stress can take a toll on your physical health, contributing to conditions such as hypertension, heart disease, and weakened immunity. Effective stress management techniques, such as mindfulness, deep breathing, and regular physical activity, are essential for maintaining physical resilience.

By assessing these areas, you can identify strengths and areas for improvement, setting the stage for developing a more resilient body.

Building a Resilient Body: Practical Tips for Enhancing Physical Health

Once you have assessed your current physical health, the next step is to implement strategies to build and maintain a resilient body. Here are practical tips for each key area:

1. **Nutrition:**
   - **Balanced Diet**: Focus on a diet that includes a variety of nutrient-dense foods. Incorporate plenty of fruits and vegetables, lean proteins (such as fish, chicken, beans, and nuts), and whole grains. Limit the intake of processed foods, sugary drinks, and excessive saturated fats.
   - **Hydration**: Drink plenty of water throughout the day. Staying hydrated is vital for maintaining energy levels, supporting digestion, and regulating body temperature.
   - **Mindful Eating**: Practice mindful eating by paying attention to your hunger and fullness cues, eating slowly, and savoring each bite. This helps prevent overeating and promotes better digestion.

2. **Exercise:**
   - **Consistency**: Establish a regular exercise routine that includes a mix of cardiovascular exercises (like running, cycling, or

swimming), strength training (such as weightlifting or bodyweight exercises), and flexibility exercises (like yoga or stretching).

- o **Gradual Progression**: Start at a level that is appropriate for your current fitness level and gradually increase the intensity and duration of your workouts. This approach prevents injury and promotes sustainable progress.
- o **Variety**: Incorporate different types of exercise to work for various muscle groups and keep your routine engaging. This could include alternating between activities like jogging, swimming, cycling, and strength training.

3. Sleep:
- o **Establish a Routine**: Go to bed and wake up at the same time each day, even on weekends. This helps regulate your body's internal clock and improves sleep quality.
- o **Sleep Environment**: Create a sleep-friendly environment by keeping your bedroom cool, dark, and quiet. Invest in a comfortable mattress and pillows, and limit exposure to screens before bedtime.
- o **Relaxation Techniques**: Practice relaxation techniques such as deep breathing, meditation, or reading before bed to help wind down and prepare for restful sleep.

4. Stress Management:

- o **Mindfulness and Meditation**: Engage in mindfulness practices or meditation to help manage stress and maintain emotional balance. These practices can reduce stress hormone levels and promote a calm, focused mind.
- o **Physical Activity**: Regular exercise is one of the most effective ways to manage stress. Physical activity releases endorphins, which act as natural stress relievers, and helps clear the mind.
- o **Social Support**: Maintain strong connections with friends and family. Social support is a key factor in resilience, providing emotional comfort and practical assistance in times of stress.

Mind-Body Connection: The Link Between Physical Health and Mental Resilience

Physical health and mental resilience are deeply interconnected. A strong body supports a strong mind, and vice versa. When we take care of our physical health, we enhance our ability to cope with stress, make better decisions, and maintain emotional stability.

1. **Exercise and Mental Health**: Regular physical activity has been shown to reduce symptoms of anxiety and depression, improve mood, and boost cognitive function. Exercise stimulates the production of endorphins and neurotransmitters

like serotonin, which help regulate mood and promote a sense of well-being.

2. **Nutrition and Mental Clarity**: A balanced diet rich in nutrients supports brain health and cognitive function. Omega-3 fatty acids, found in fish and nuts, are particularly beneficial for brain health, while vitamins and minerals like B vitamins, vitamin D, and magnesium support overall mental clarity and energy levels.

3. **Sleep and Cognitive Function**: Adequate sleep is crucial for cognitive function, memory consolidation, and emotional regulation. Lack of sleep can impair decision-making, increase irritability, and reduce the ability to cope with stress. Prioritizing good sleep hygiene supports both physical health and mental resilience.

4. **Stress Management and Physical Health**: Effective stress management techniques not only protect mental health but also prevent the physical toll that chronic stress can take on the body. Practices like mindfulness, meditation, and regular physical activity help keep stress levels in check, promoting overall resilience.

8.4 Reflect and Apply

Personal Reflection

As you consider your physical health practices, reflect on the following questions:

- Are you nourishing your body with a balanced diet, or are there areas where you could improve?
- How consistent is your exercise routine? Are you incorporating a variety of physical activities that challenge and strengthen your body?
- Are you getting enough sleep? If not, what changes can you make to improve your sleep quality?
- How do you currently manage stress? Are there additional strategies you could implement to better handle stress and protect your physical and mental health?

Action Steps: Integrating Physical Well-being into Resilience Plans

To strengthen your physical resilience and, in turn, your overall resilience, consider taking the following action steps:

1. **Create a Health Plan**: Develop a personalized health plan that includes balanced nutrition, regular exercise, and adequate sleep. Set realistic goals and track your progress to stay motivated.
2. **Schedule Regular Exercise**: Commit to a regular exercise routine that fits your lifestyle. Whether it's morning runs, evening yoga, or weekend hikes, find activities you enjoy and make them a priority.
3. **Prioritize Sleep**: Establish a consistent sleep schedule and create a sleep-friendly environment. Consider setting a bedtime alarm to remind yourself to wind down and prepare for sleep.
4. **Practice Mindfulness**: Incorporate mindfulness practices into your daily routine to manage stress

and maintain emotional balance. This could include morning meditation, deep breathing exercises during breaks, or a mindful walk after work.

5. **Seek Support**: Engage with a support network of friends, family, or a fitness community to stay accountable and motivated in your health journey. Share your goals and challenges with others who can provide encouragement and guidance.

By reflecting on your current practices and taking concrete steps to enhance your physical health, you can build a resilient body that supports your mental and emotional well-being. Integrating physical well-being into your resilience plan ensures that you are well-prepared to face life's challenges with strength, energy, and confidence.

CHAPTER GEM ELEMENTS

- ❖ **Physical Activity as a Foundation of Resilience**: Recognize physical health as a key component of resilience and engage in regular physical activity.
- ❖ **Healthy Habits and Regular Hygiene**: Develop and maintain healthy habits and keep regular hygiene practices that support long-term physical well-being.
- ❖ **Lead by Example in Physical Effort**: Demonstrate resilience through physical effort and discipline, setting an example for others.

Chapter 9: Navigating New Horizons

Be Open to Innovation and The Unknown

In today's rapidly changing world, resilience is no longer just about surviving difficulties but also about thriving in the face of new opportunities and challenges. "Navigating New Horizons" in the MLRM framework expands beyond the digital realm, focusing on an openness to innovation, the unknown, and the evolving landscapes that shape our future. True resilience means embracing change, adapting to shifts in the environment, and being open to new ways of thinking and problem-solving.

Just as the Prophet Muhammad (PBUH) demonstrated adaptability and foresight in his life, navigating uncharted territories with wisdom and clarity, we too are called to approach new horizons with courage and a willingness to learn. Whether it's technological advancements, societal transformations, or unforeseen challenges, resilience involves not only reacting to change but proactively seeking it. Being open to innovation means understanding that the world will continue to evolve, and those who are adaptable will not only survive but lead.

At the core of this idea is the principle that resilience is about growth; being open to new experiences, ideas, and methods that can enhance our personal, organizational, and communal strength. By embracing this mindset, we set ourselves up to build stronger systems, whether in the form of new technologies, innovative leadership approaches, or community-driven solutions that meet the needs of an ever-changing world.

The Digital World - Building Digital and Virtual Resilience

A prime example of navigating new horizons is the digital revolution. As technology continues to reshape communication, work, and social interaction, building digital resilience is essential. The digital world presents opportunities for innovation, but it also requires critical thinking, adaptability, and ethical usage. From learning to master communication tools to protecting personal data and adapting to remote work environments, the digital shift is a reflection of how resilience must evolve in line with new challenges. Embracing this new frontier strengthens our ability to navigate future shifts and fosters a mindset ready for continuous growth and innovation.

In today's world, the digital realm is both a vast resource and a significant challenge. While technology connects us and provides unprecedented access to information, it also presents unique challenges like information overload, cyberbullying, and digital distractions. To thrive in this environment, it is essential to develop digital resilience; the ability to navigate and respond effectively to the demands of the digital age. In this chapter, we will explore the challenges of the digital world, the importance of digital resilience, and draw parallels from the Prophet Muhammad's communication strategies to guide our approach.

9.1 The Challenges of the Digital Age

Digital Resilience: Understanding the Challenges

The digital era brings with it several challenges that require us to build resilience in new ways. Some of the most pressing issues include:

1. **Information Overload**: The sheer volume of information available online can be overwhelming. Every day, we are bombarded with news, social media updates, advertisements, and emails, making it difficult to focus and prioritize what truly matters. Information overload can lead to decision fatigue, stress, and even a sense of helplessness.

2. **Cyberbullying**: The anonymity of the internet allows for harmful behavior to proliferate, including cyberbullying. Unlike traditional bullying, which has physical boundaries, cyberbullying can occur anytime and anywhere, often leaving victims feeling trapped and isolated. The emotional toll of cyberbullying can be severe, impacting mental health and overall well-being.

3. **Digital Distractions**: The digital world is filled with distractions that can disrupt productivity and focus. From social media notifications to endless scrolling, these distractions can erode our attention span and reduce our ability to engage deeply with tasks or ideas. Over time, constant digital distractions can impair cognitive function and diminish the quality of our work and relationships.

Why It's Important: The Necessity of Digital Resilience

In a tech-driven world, digital resilience is not just beneficial; it's essential. Here's why:

1. **Adaptation to Change**: Technology is constantly evolving, and so are the challenges that come with it. Developing digital resilience enables us to adapt to these changes, ensuring we can continue to function effectively in both our personal and professional lives.

2. **Protection of Mental Health**: By building digital resilience, we can safeguard our mental health against the negative impacts of the digital world, such as stress, anxiety, and depression. This involves setting boundaries, practicing mindfulness, and engaging in digital detoxes to maintain a healthy relationship with technology.

3. **Empowerment Through Knowledge**: Digital resilience empowers us to critically evaluate the information we encounter online, discern between truth and misinformation, and make informed decisions. This is crucial in an era where misinformation can spread rapidly and influence public opinion, behavior, and even policy.

4. **Effective Communication**: In a world where communication increasingly takes place online, digital resilience ensures that we can express ourselves clearly, build meaningful connections, and engage in productive dialogue, even in the face of challenges like cyberbullying or misinformation.

9.2 Parallels from the Prophet's Communication

Drawing from the life of the Prophet Muhammad, we find valuable lessons that can guide our approach to digital resilience. His communication strategies, although from a pre-digital era, offer timeless wisdom that can be applied to navigating the complexities of the digital world.

Effective Communication: Lessons from the Prophet Muhammad

One of the key aspects of digital resilience is the ability to communicate effectively in the online world. The Prophet Muhammad's use of letters to communicate with distant rulers serves as an early example of strategic communication in a connected world.

The Use of Letters for Communication: The Prophet Muhammad (PBUH) strategically used letters to communicate with distant rulers, spreading his message across vast distances. This approach highlights the importance of adapting to the best available communication technology of the time. In today's context, this means embracing digital tools for communication, but doing so with intentionality and purpose. The Prophet's example reminds us that resilience in the digital world involves not just the use of technology, but the thoughtful and effective use of it to maintain clarity, integrity, and connection. Source: "Al-Sirah al-Nabawiyyah (The Prophetic Biography)"

Navigating Information Overload: The Prophet's Discernment

In the face of the overwhelming amount of information online, critical thinking is essential. The Prophet Muhammad's discernment in distinguishing truth from falsehood offers a powerful parallel for navigating information overload in the digital age.

The Protection of Information: The Prophet Muhammad (PBUH) placed great emphasis on the protection of information, ensuring the accurate transmission of the Qur'an and Hadith. This careful preservation of knowledge reflects the importance of safeguarding the integrity of information. In the digital era, this translates to the need for cybersecurity and critical thinking to protect against misinformation and data breaches. Just as the Prophet ensured the authenticity of sacred texts, we must critically evaluate the information we encounter online and protect our digital data. Source: "Ar-Raheeq Al-Makhtum (The Sealed Nectar)"

Delegation and Specialization: Managing Digital Complexities

In managing the complexities of the digital world, effective delegation and specialization are crucial. The Prophet Muhammad's delegation of tasks to his companions, based on their strengths and expertise, provides a model for navigating digital challenges.

The Delegation of Tasks: The Prophet Muhammad (PBUH) effectively delegated tasks to his companions, recognizing their individual strengths and areas of expertise. This approach ensured that each task was handled by the most capable individual, leading to successful outcomes. In the digital world, managing the vast array of information and tasks can be overwhelming. By delegating responsibilities, whether in a professional setting or in managing personal digital spaces, we can focus on what we do best and build resilience by not overburdening ourselves. Source: "Al-Sirah al-Nabawiyyah (The Prophetic Biography)"

The Prophet's Mastery of Language and Oral Tradition

In a time long before digital communication, the Prophet Muhammad (PBUH) harnessed the power of oral tradition and poetry to convey his message with impact. His understanding of language as a tool for influence mirrors the way modern leaders use digital content creation today. The Prophet's ability to craft compelling narratives and engage his audience resonates with the need for effective storytelling in the virtual space. Just as he leveraged the power of words to shape minds and hearts, we too must master digital storytelling and communication strategies to build resilience in an increasingly online world. It's about creating narratives that resonate deeply, foster connection, and inspire action. Source: "Fada'il al-A'mal"

The Preservation of the Qur'an through Memory and Recitation

Before the Qur'an was written down, it was safeguarded through memorization and recitation, a method that ensured its preservation across generations. The Prophet Muhammad (PBUH) emphasized the importance of committing the Qur'an to memory, recognizing that true preservation lies not in material forms but in the minds and hearts of people. This is a powerful analogy for data protection in the digital age. As we navigate a world where information can be easily lost or corrupted, the resilience of the Prophet's approach teaches us that safeguarding critical data; whether it's personal, organizational, or societal; requires vigilance, attention to detail, and a long-term strategy. In the digital space, resilience is about protecting what matters most with the same diligence and foresight. Source: "Al-Sirah al-Nabawiyyah"

The Prophet's Strategic Use of Letters to Distant Leaders

The Prophet Muhammad's use of letter writing to communicate with distant rulers demonstrates a keen understanding of diplomacy, strategy, and long-range communication. In a world without instant messaging or email, he carefully crafted his letters, ensuring clarity and maintaining respect, even with those far from his immediate sphere of influence. This historical example is remarkably relevant in today's digital diplomacy, where communication happens across continents at the click of a button. The Prophet's letters remind us that digital resilience requires clarity, respect, and precision in online interactions, especially when bridging geographical and cultural divides. Today, effective online communication; whether in business, diplomacy, or personal relationships; is a cornerstone of resilience in the digital world. *Source: "Kitab al-Samarkandiyya"*

Key Takeaways

1. **Digital resilience is essential in today's tech-driven world**, enabling us to adapt to changes,

protect our mental health, and communicate effectively online.

2. **Effective communication in the digital age requires thoughtful use of technology**: Drawing on the Prophet Muhammad's strategic communication methods as a model for purposeful and clear interactions. In the digital age, effective communication requires both the adoption of new tools and the discernment to use them wisely. By following the Prophet's example, we can build resilience by ensuring our digital interactions are purposeful and aligned with our values.

3. **Critical thinking is crucial for navigating information overload**, following the Prophet's example of safeguarding information to protect against misinformation and cyber threats.

4. **Delegation and specialization are key to managing digital complexities**: Allowing us to focus on our strengths and avoid becoming overwhelmed by the vastness of the digital world. Building digital resilience involves recognizing when to delegate tasks and when to specialize in specific areas. By following the Prophet's example of delegation, we can manage the complexities of the digital world more effectively, ensuring that we remain focused, productive, and resilient.

5. **Mastering Communication:** The Prophet's use of poetry and oral tradition to spread his message shows the importance of mastering communication tools. In the digital age, effective communication is

key to building and maintaining resilience in virtual environments.

6. **Data Protection:** The Prophet's emphasis on the accurate transmission of the Qur'an through memorization parallels the modern need for cybersecurity and data protection. Safeguarding information is essential for maintaining resilience in the digital world. Resilience in the digital world involves not only protecting our personal information but also critically assessing the credibility of the content we consume. By following the Prophet's example of information protection, we can strengthen our digital resilience against misinformation and cyber threats.

7. **Diplomatic Communication:** The Prophet's strategic use of letters to distant leaders highlights the importance of clear and respectful communication in building virtual networks. In the digital age, diplomacy and clarity in communication are critical for fostering strong, resilient relationships.

Reflection: Digital resilience is built through effective communication, data protection, and diplomatic engagement. Master the tools of the digital world to strengthen your virtual presence and ensure long-term resilience.

By integrating these lessons into our digital practices, we can build the resilience needed to navigate the challenges of the digital era with confidence and clarity.

Building Digital Resilience

As the digital world becomes increasingly integral to our lives, the need for digital resilience has never been more critical. Digital resilience involves not just adapting to the rapid pace of technological change but also managing our digital consumption, maintaining cyber wellness, and developing digital literacy. We will delve into strategies for building digital resilience, providing practical tools and actionable advice to help navigate the challenges of the digital era.

9.3 Building Digital Resilience

Managing Digital Consumption

In an era of constant connectivity, managing digital consumption is vital for maintaining balance and focus. The overwhelming flood of information, notifications, and content can easily lead to burnout and stress if not carefully managed. Here are some strategies for controlling digital consumption:

1. **Set Clear Boundaries**: Establishing clear boundaries around digital use is essential. This might include setting specific times for checking emails, social media, or news, and sticking to them. For instance, you could designate the first hour of your day as a "no-screen" time, allowing you to start your day with intention rather than distraction. Similarly, setting "digital curfews" in the evening can help improve sleep quality and reduce stress.

2. **Practice Digital Detoxes**: Regularly disconnecting from digital devices can significantly

enhance mental clarity and reduce stress. A digital detox might involve unplugging for a weekend, spending time in nature, or simply turning off your phone for a few hours each day. The goal is to give your mind a break from the constant stimulation of the digital world, allowing you to recharge and refocus.

3. **Mindful Consumption**: Be intentional about the content you consume. Instead of mindlessly scrolling through social media or binge-watching videos, choose content that enriches your mind or contributes to your well-being. Follow accounts that inspire or educate, and limit exposure to content that triggers negative emotions or anxiety.

4. **Use Technology Wisely**: Tools like screen time trackers and app usage monitors can help you become more aware of your digital habits. By analyzing your usage patterns, you can make informed decisions about where to cut back and how to optimize your time online.

Reflection: Managing digital consumption is crucial for maintaining mental clarity and reducing stress. By setting boundaries, practicing digital detoxes, and being mindful about what we consume, we can build a healthier relationship with technology.

Cyber Wellness: Maintaining Mental and Emotional Well-being Online

The digital world can have a profound impact on our mental and emotional well-being. From cyberbullying to the anxiety of constantly being "on," the online environment can be challenging. Cyber wellness involves adopting strategies to protect and enhance our mental and emotional health in the digital space.

1. **Emotional Boundaries**: Establish emotional boundaries online just as you would in real life. This might mean unfollowing accounts that cause stress or anxiety, avoiding engaging in online arguments, or limiting exposure to distressing news. Protecting your mental space is key to maintaining emotional resilience in the digital world.

2. **Mindful Interaction**: Engage with others online in a way that is thoughtful and positive. Before posting or commenting, consider whether your contribution is constructive and kind. This not only helps create a more positive online environment but also reduces the likelihood of becoming involved in negative interactions that can drain emotional energy.

3. **Digital Support Networks**: Build a network of supportive, positive influences online. Follow accounts that uplift, educate, and inspire you. Engage in online communities that share your interests and values, and seek out spaces where you can connect with others in meaningful, supportive ways.

4. **Stress Management**: Incorporate stress management techniques into your digital routine. This might include taking regular breaks, practicing deep breathing exercises, or using meditation apps designed to help you unwind and relax. By

integrating these practices into your digital life, you can mitigate the negative impacts of stress and maintain your mental and emotional well-being.

Reflection: Cyber wellness is about maintaining mental and emotional health in the online environment. By setting emotional boundaries, interacting mindfully, building positive support networks, and managing stress, we can navigate the digital world with resilience.

Digital Literacy: Navigating the Digital World with Confidence

Digital literacy is the ability to critically evaluate and effectively use digital tools and information. In an age where misinformation is rampant, and the line between truth and falsehood can be blurred, digital literacy is essential for building resilience.

1. **Critical Thinking**: Develop the habit of questioning the information you encounter online. Look for credible sources, check the authenticity of information before sharing, and be aware of biases that may influence how information is presented. Critical thinking skills are your first line of defense against misinformation and manipulation in the digital world.

2. **Understanding Digital Footprints**: Be aware of the lasting impact of your online actions. Everything you post, share, or comment on contributes to your digital footprint. Understanding this helps you make more conscious decisions about what you

share and how you interact online, protecting your privacy and reputation.

3. **Privacy Awareness**: Take steps to protect your personal information online. This includes using strong, unique passwords, being cautious about sharing personal details, and being aware of the privacy settings on the platforms you use. Cybersecurity is a key component of digital literacy, helping you safeguard your data and maintain control over your online presence.

4. **Staying Updated**: The digital landscape is constantly evolving, and staying informed about new technologies, platforms, and security threats is crucial. Regularly update your knowledge of digital tools and best practices to ensure you're navigating the digital world safely and effectively.

Reflection: Digital literacy is essential for building resilience in the digital age. By honing critical thinking skills, understanding digital footprints, prioritizing privacy, and staying informed, we can navigate the digital world with confidence and integrity.

9.4 Reflect and Apply

Personal Reflection: Evaluating Your Digital Habits

Before you can build digital resilience, it's important to assess your current digital habits. Reflect on the following questions:

- How much time do I spend online each day? Is it productive, or do I often feel overwhelmed or distracted?
- Do I have clear boundaries around my digital use, or do I find it difficult to disconnect?
- How does my online activity impact my mental and emotional well-being? Am I engaging in positive interactions, or do I frequently feel stressed or anxious after spending time online?
- Do I critically evaluate the information I consume, or do I sometimes share or believe information without verifying its authenticity?
- Am I aware of my digital footprint and taking steps to protect my privacy online?

This self-assessment will help you identify areas where you might need to make changes to improve your digital resilience.

Reflection: Reflecting on your digital habits is the first step in building digital resilience. By honestly evaluating how you interact with the digital world, you can identify areas for improvement and set the foundation for healthier digital practices.

Action Steps: Building Digital Resilience

Based on your reflection, consider taking the following action steps to build digital resilience:

1. **Set Digital Boundaries**: Establish clear limits on when and how you use digital devices. This might include setting specific times for checking emails or

social media, taking regular digital detoxes, or implementing screen-free zones in your home.

2. **Practice Cyber Wellness**: Focus on maintaining your mental and emotional health online. This includes setting emotional boundaries, engaging in positive interactions, and using stress management techniques to reduce the negative impacts of online activity.

3. **Enhance Digital Literacy**: Invest time in developing your digital literacy skills. Learn to critically evaluate online information, understand the implications of your digital footprint, and prioritize your privacy and security online.

4. **Monitor and Adjust**: Regularly assess your digital habits and make adjustments as needed. As technology evolves, so should your strategies for managing digital consumption and maintaining cyber wellness.

Reflection: Building digital resilience requires intentional action. By setting boundaries, practicing cyber wellness, enhancing digital literacy, and regularly assessing your habits, you can navigate the digital world with confidence and resilience.

By integrating these strategies into your daily life, you can develop the digital resilience necessary to thrive in the digital age. The challenges of the online world are real, but with the right tools and mindset, you can navigate them effectively, maintaining both your mental and emotional well-being.

CHAPTER GEM ELEMENTS

- ❖ **Navigating New Horizons**: Embracing Innovation and Change. True resilience is about embracing new opportunities, adapting to evolving challenges, and proactively seeking growth in all aspects of life.

- ❖ **Digital Resilience:** In today's tech-driven world, resilience means adapting to digital changes, protecting mental health, and maintaining thoughtful online interactions.

- ❖ **Purposeful Communication:** Engage in clear, value-driven digital communication to foster resilience, just as strategic communication was key in historical leadership.

- ❖ **Critical Thinking:** Navigate information overload by applying critical thinking, safeguarding against misinformation and digital threats.

- ❖ **Delegation in the Digital Age:** Focus on your strengths and delegate tasks to manage digital complexities effectively, ensuring sustained productivity and resilience.

- ❖ **Mastery of Digital Tools:** Master communication tools, using them wisely to strengthen your presence in virtual environments.

- ❖ **Data Protection:** Protect personal information and ensure the credibility of digital content, paralleling the safeguarding of knowledge in traditional systems.

Chapter 10: Financial Freedom

Achieving Economic Resilience

Financial resilience is a cornerstone of overall well-being. It's the ability to withstand and recover from economic shocks, ensuring that financial stress doesn't derail your life. In today's complex financial landscape, achieving economic resilience requires a combination of financial literacy, ethical practices, and strategic planning. This chapter will explore the foundations of financial resilience, drawing on the wisdom of Prophet Muhammad's approach to commerce and wealth management.

10.1 The Foundation of Financial Resilience

Why Financial Stability Matters

Financial stability is not just about having enough money to meet your basic needs; it's about creating a secure foundation that allows you to pursue your goals, take risks, and face challenges with confidence. Financial security underpins resilience in several ways:

1. **Reduces Stress and Anxiety**: Financial instability is one of the leading causes of stress and anxiety. When you're constantly worried about money, it's hard to focus on other aspects of life, whether it's building relationships, advancing in your career, or taking care of your health. Financial stability provides peace of mind, freeing you from the constant worry of making ends meet.

2. **Enables Long-Term Planning**: Without financial stability, it's challenging to think beyond the immediate future. Economic resilience allows you to plan for the long term, whether that's saving for retirement, investing in education, or starting a business. It provides the freedom to make choices that align with your values and aspirations, rather than being dictated by financial necessity.

3. **Facilitates Personal Growth**: When you're not preoccupied with financial survival, you have the mental and emotional bandwidth to invest in personal growth. Whether it's learning new skills, pursuing hobbies, or engaging in community service, financial stability allows you to focus on what truly matters in life.

Reflection: Financial stability is crucial for overall resilience, reducing stress, enabling long-term planning, and facilitating personal growth. It's not just about having money, but about having the freedom to live a life aligned with your values and goals.

The Impact of Financial Stress

The psychological toll of financial instability is significant. When financial stress becomes chronic, it can lead to a range of negative outcomes, both mentally and physically:

1. **Mental Health Struggles**: Persistent financial stress is linked to anxiety, depression, and even suicidal thoughts. The constant pressure to meet financial obligations can lead to feelings of

helplessness and hopelessness, eroding mental resilience.

2. **Strained Relationships**: Money problems are a common source of conflict in relationships. Financial stress can lead to arguments, resentment, and even the breakdown of marriages and partnerships. The strain of financial instability doesn't just affect your own well-being; it can also impact those around you.

3. **Poor Physical Health**: Financial stress can manifest physically, leading to issues like insomnia, headaches, and weakened immune function. Over time, the stress hormone cortisol can contribute to serious health conditions like heart disease and high blood pressure.

Reflection: Financial stress has far-reaching effects on mental, emotional, and physical well-being. Addressing financial instability is crucial for maintaining overall resilience and quality of life.

10.2 Financial Wisdom from the Prophet

Business Ethics: Prophet Muhammad's Ethical Approach to Commerce

Prophet Muhammad's life offers timeless lessons in financial resilience, particularly in the realm of business ethics. His approach to commerce was rooted in honesty, integrity, and fairness; principles that remain relevant in today's economic environment.

The Prophet's Early Career as a Merchant

Before his prophethood, Muhammad (PBUH) was a successful merchant known for his exceptional honesty and integrity. His reputation for fairness and trustworthiness attracted customers and built strong business relationships. This ethical approach to commerce provided him with financial stability, allowing him the freedom to later focus on his prophetic mission.

This story underscores the importance of ethical financial practices in building economic resilience. By conducting business with honesty and integrity, you not only gain the trust of others but also create a stable financial foundation that can support you through life's challenges.

Reflection: Ethical business practices, such as honesty and integrity, are essential for achieving financial resilience. These principles build trust, foster long-term success, and create a stable foundation for navigating economic challenges.

Fair Trade Principles: The Prophet's Commitment to Ethical Wealth

Prophet Muhammad (PBUH) was also committed to fair trade and the ethical distribution of wealth. His teachings emphasized the importance of fairness and justice in financial transactions, ensuring that wealth was acquired and distributed in a way that benefited the entire community.

The Management of Wealth in Medina

Upon arriving in Medina, Prophet Muhammad (PBUH) instituted systems of charity (Zakat) and wealth distribution that ensured economic stability within the community. By encouraging the wealthy to share their resources and ensuring that everyone had access to basic needs, the Prophet created an economically resilient community that could withstand external pressures and internal challenges.

This story illustrates the power of fair-trade principles in achieving economic resilience. By focusing on the ethical distribution of wealth and ensuring that financial transactions are just and fair, we can create a more resilient and equitable society.

Reflection: Fair-trade and ethical wealth distribution are key components of financial resilience. By ensuring that financial practices are just and equitable, we can build a stronger, more resilient community.

The Prophet's Prohibition of Hoarding Wealth

This is could sound similar to the above point, but it is actually another dimension of it. In a world driven by accumulation, the Prophet Muhammad (PBUH) emphasized the moral and economic hazards of hoarding wealth. He instilled in his followers the practice of *Zakat*; a system of mandatory charity that ensured wealth was continuously circulated within the community. This wasn't just about redistributing wealth; it was about fostering a collective resilience. By ensuring that resources flowed rather than stagnated, the Prophet prevented wealth disparities from corroding the fabric of society. Wealth wasn't meant to sit idly in vaults; it was meant to be a force that strengthened the entire community. *Source: Kitab al-Samarkandiyya*

Ethical Wealth Management: The Prophet's prohibition of hoarding wealth and encouragement of charity (Zakat) highlights the importance of ethical financial practices. Economic resilience is achieved by ensuring wealth circulates fairly, supporting both personal and community well-being.

The Prohibition of Usury (Riba)

One of the most significant financial teachings of the Prophet Muhammad (PBUH) was his prohibition of usury (Riba). This practice, which involves charging excessive interest on loans, was seen as exploitative and harmful to economic stability. The prohibition of usury was aimed at preventing financial exploitation and ensuring fairness in financial transactions.

The lesson here is clear: Ethical financial principles, such as avoiding exploitation and ensuring fairness, are crucial for long-term economic resilience. By adhering to these principles, we can create a financial system that supports the well-being of all members of society, rather than just a privileged few.

Reflection: Avoiding exploitative financial practices, such as usury, is essential for achieving financial resilience. By promoting fairness and justice in financial transactions, we can build a more stable and equitable economic system.

The Prophet's Trust in God during Times of Hardship

Even in times of financial hardship, the Prophet Muhammad (PBUH) exhibited remarkable patience and unwavering trust in divine provision. He lived through periods of extreme hardship, yet his faith remained unshaken. This wasn't passive resignation; it was a profound spiritual resilience that teaches us that financial freedom isn't solely tied to material wealth. True economic resilience comes from the strength to endure hardship with grace, knowing that wealth is temporary, but faith and trust in a greater plan provide a stable foundation. *Source: Fada'il al-A'mal*

The Prophet's Management of War Booty

The Prophet Muhammad's leadership extended to the fair and equitable distribution of war booty, ensuring that wealth reached all segments of society; even those who didn't directly contribute to the battlefield. His approach ensured that women, children, and the vulnerable were not left behind. This fairness in wealth management prevented societal divisions, reinforcing economic resilience at every level. It wasn't just about distribution; it was about reinforcing trust and unity within the community, ensuring that wealth became a tool for collective upliftment rather than a source of division. *Source: Al-Sirah al-Nabawiyyah*

The Prophet's teachings offer a timeless blueprint: true financial resilience isn't built on personal gain but on fostering a system where everyone benefits. Wealth, when distributed justly, becomes a source of strength for the entire society.

The Prophet's Crisis Management and Saving Strategy

One remarkable example of Prophet Muhammad's foresight and practical approach to resilience is found in his practice of saving a year's worth of food for his wives and family. This wasn't simply about stockpiling; it was a profound strategy rooted in the understanding that resilience isn't just about surviving the unexpected, but about preparing for it.

In Islamic texts such as Sahih Bukhari, it's mentioned that the Prophet would set aside provisions for his household to last an entire year. This wasn't an act of excess or fear, but of calculated preparation. The Prophet lived in a society where resources were often scarce, and survival depended on the ability to think ahead. By securing food supplies for his family, he demonstrated the balance between trusting in Allah (Tawakkul) and taking practical steps to ensure well-being.

This strategy of saving provisions can be seen as an early form of crisis management. Instead of waiting for the crisis to hit, the Prophet Muhammad (PBUH) ensured that his family could withstand potential disruptions, whether due to drought, war, or economic hardship. His actions show us that resilience is not just about enduring the tough times but about building a buffer to handle them when they inevitably come.

This example from the life of Prophet Muhammad (PBUH) speaks to a broader principle: true resilience is proactive, not reactive. You don't wait until you're out of resources to find a solution; you prepare in advance so that when adversity strikes, you have the reserves to navigate through it smoothly.

Financial resilience is not just about accumulating wealth; it's about creating a stable foundation that allows you to navigate life's challenges with confidence and integrity. By adopting ethical financial practices, such as those exemplified by Prophet Muhammad, we can build a financial system that supports not only our individual well-being but also the well-being of our communities.

Key Takeaways:

- **Financial Stability**: Crucial for reducing stress, enabling long-term planning, and fostering personal growth.
- **Impact of Financial Stress**: Significant toll on mental, emotional, and physical health, emphasizing the need for financial resilience.
- **Ethical Financial Practices**: Honesty, integrity, and fairness are key to building trust and achieving long-term financial success.
- **Fair Trade and Wealth Distribution**: Ensuring just and equitable financial transactions creates a more resilient community.
- **Avoiding Exploitation**: Ethical principles, such as the prohibition of usury, are essential for maintaining economic stability and resilience.
- **Trust in Provision:** The Prophet's patience during times of hardship teaches that financial resilience is also about trust and contentment. True

economic freedom comes not just from wealth but from a mindset of sufficiency and gratitude.

- **Equitable Distribution:** The Prophet's management of war booty, ensuring even non-combatants received their share, underscores the importance of fairness in financial dealings. Equitable distribution of resources strengthens the economic resilience of the entire community.

- **Crisis management:** True resilience lies in being proactive rather than reactive. Don't wait until you're out of resources to seek a solution; prepare in advance. Set aside some savings to ensure you're ready for unexpected challenges.

Reflection: Financial resilience is rooted in ethical practices, trust in provision, and fairness in distribution. Manage your finances with integrity, cultivate contentment, and ensure equitable wealth distribution to achieve true economic freedom.

By integrating these principles into our financial practices, we can achieve true financial freedom; one that not only secures our own future but also contributes to the greater good.

10.3 Building Economic Resilience

Financial Literacy: The Cornerstone of Economic Resilience

Financial literacy is the foundation upon which economic resilience is built. It involves understanding basic financial principles; such as budgeting, saving, and investing; and knowing how to apply them in your daily life.

1. **Budgeting**: Creating and sticking to a budget is the first step in managing your finances. A budget helps you track your income and expenses, ensuring that you live within your means. To build economic resilience, it's important to budget not only for regular expenses but also to set aside funds for emergencies and future goals.

    o   **Tip**: Use the 50/30/20 rule as a starting point: allocate 50% of your income to necessities, 30% to discretionary spending, and 20% to savings and debt repayment. This simple framework can help you create a balanced financial plan.

2. **Saving**: Saving money is crucial for building financial security. Having an emergency fund can protect you from unexpected expenses, such as medical bills or car repairs, without going into debt. Additionally, saving for long-term goals, like buying a home or retirement, ensures that you're prepared for the future.

    o   **Tip**: Aim to save at least three to six months' worth of living expenses in an emergency fund. Automate your savings by setting up regular transfers from your checking account to a savings account.

3. **Investing**: Investing allows your money to grow over time, helping you build wealth and achieve long-term financial goals. Understanding different types of investments; such as stocks, bonds, and real

estate; can help you make informed decisions that align with your risk tolerance and financial objectives.

- o **Tip**: **Tip**: Begin with low-risk investments if you're new to investing. As you build confidence and gain knowledge, you can gradually explore more diverse investment opportunities.

Reflection: Financial literacy is essential for economic resilience. By mastering budgeting, saving, and investing, you can create a solid financial foundation that supports your long-term goals and protects you from financial shocks.

Creating a Financial Plan: A Roadmap to Resilience

A resilient financial plan is more than just a budget or a savings account; it's a comprehensive strategy that covers all aspects of your financial life. Here's how to build one:

1. **Set Clear Goals**: Start by defining your financial goals. These can be short-term (e.g., paying off debt), medium-term (e.g., buying a home), and long-term (e.g., retirement). Having clear goals gives you direction and motivation to stick to your financial plan.
   - o **Tip**: Use the SMART criteria (Specific, Measurable, Achievable, Relevant, Time-bound) to set your goals. For example, instead of saying, "I want to save money," say,

"I want to save $10,000 for a down payment on a house within the next two years."

2. **Develop a Savings and Investment Strategy**: Based on your goals, create a plan for saving and investing. Determine how much you need to save each month to reach your goals and decide where to invest your money to maximize growth while managing risk.

   o **Tip**: Diversify your investments across different asset classes to reduce risk. Don't put all your money into one type of investment; instead, spread it out across stocks, bonds, real estate, and other opportunities.

3. **Plan for Emergencies**: Ensure your financial plan includes provisions for emergencies. This could mean having an emergency fund, appropriate insurance coverage, and a plan for managing debt.

   o **Tip**: Review your insurance policies (e.g., health, home, auto) to ensure you're adequately covered. Insurance is a key part of financial resilience, as it protects you from significant financial losses.

4. **Review and Adjust**: A financial plan is not static; it needs to be reviewed and adjusted regularly. Life changes; such as marriage, children, or a new job; can impact your financial situation, so it's important to update your plan accordingly.

   o **Tip**: Set a reminder to review your financial plan at least once a year. During this review, assess your progress toward your goals, make any necessary adjustments, and ensure your investments are still aligned with your risk tolerance.

Reflection: A resilient financial plan is a comprehensive strategy that covers all aspects of your financial life, from setting clear goals to planning for emergencies. Regularly reviewing and adjusting your plan ensures that you stay on track to achieve your financial objectives.

Ethical Wealth-Building: Following the Prophet's Approach

Building wealth is not just about accumulating money; it's about doing so in a way that aligns with your values and contributes to the greater good. Prophet Muhammad's approach to wealth-building was deeply rooted in ethics, and his principles can guide us in our modern financial lives.

1. **Honesty and Integrity**: The Prophet was known for his honesty and integrity in business dealings. He built a reputation for fairness, which not only earned him financial success but also respect and trust. In today's world, maintaining honesty and integrity in financial transactions is just as important.
   - **Tip**: Practice transparency in all your financial dealings, whether in business or personal finance. This includes being honest in negotiations, honoring your commitments, and avoiding deceptive practices.

2. **Fair Trade and Avoiding Exploitation**: The Prophet emphasized the importance of fair trade and prohibited exploitative practices like usury (Riba). Building wealth ethically means ensuring that your financial practices are just and do not harm others.

   o **Tip**: Avoid investments or business practices that exploit others or are harmful to society. Instead, focus on ethical investments that contribute to positive social or environmental outcomes.

3. **Charity and Generosity**: Wealth, in the Prophet's view, was not just for personal gain but also for the benefit of the community. Zakat, or charity, was a key component of his economic teachings. Building wealth ethically involves giving back to those in need and contributing to the well-being of society.

   o **Tip**: Incorporate charitable giving into your financial plan. This could be through regular donations to causes you care about, setting up a charitable fund, or volunteering your time and skills to help others.

Reflection: Ethical wealth-building involves following principles of honesty, integrity, and fairness. By aligning your financial practices with these values, you not only achieve economic resilience but also contribute positively to society.

10.4 Reflect and Apply

Building economic resilience requires both self-reflection and action. It's important to regularly evaluate your financial practices to ensure they align with your goals and values.

Personal Reflection

1. **Assess Your Financial Habits**: Reflect on your current financial habits. Are you budgeting effectively? Are you saving and investing with a clear plan in mind? Are your financial practices aligned with your ethical values?
   o **Prompt**: Consider writing down your financial goals and the steps you're currently taking to achieve them. Are there areas where you could improve or adjust your approach?
2. **Evaluate Your Ethical Standards**: Think about the ethical standards you apply to your financial decisions. Are you conducting your financial affairs with honesty and integrity? Are you making decisions that not only benefit you but also contribute to the greater good?
   o **Prompt**: Reflect on recent financial decisions you've made. Were they in line with your ethical values? If not, what changes could you make in the future?

Reflection: Regular reflection on your financial practices ensures that they remain aligned with your goals and values, helping you build true economic resilience.

Action Steps

1. **Improve Your Financial Literacy**: Commit to learning more about personal finance. Read books, take online courses, or consult with a financial advisor to deepen your understanding of budgeting, saving, investing, and ethical wealth-building.
    o   **Action**: Set a goal to learn about one new financial concept each month. This could be anything from understanding compound interest to exploring socially responsible investing.
2. **Create or Revise Your Financial Plan**: If you don't have a financial plan, start building one today. If you already have one, take the time to review and update it. Ensure that your plan includes clear goals, a savings and investment strategy, and provisions for emergencies.
    o   **Action**: Schedule a specific time to work on your financial plan, and set a reminder to review it annually.
3. **Align Your Financial Practices with Your Values**: Make a conscious effort to ensure that your financial practices reflect your ethical values. This might involve avoiding certain types of investments, increasing your charitable giving, or committing to fair trade practices.
    o   **Action**: Identify one area where you can better align your financial practices with your values, and take concrete steps to make that change.

Reflection: Taking actionable steps to improve your financial literacy, create a resilient financial plan, and align your financial practices with your values is crucial for achieving long-term economic resilience.

In the pursuit of financial freedom and economic resilience, it is essential to build a robust understanding of financial management, create a strategic financial plan, and adhere to ethical wealth-building practices. This chapter explores practical strategies for enhancing financial literacy, developing a resilient financial plan, and building wealth ethically, all while drawing parallels to the ethical principles exemplified by Prophet Muhammad.

Economic resilience is about more than just surviving financial hardships; it's about thriving despite them. It's the ability to manage your finances in a way that prepares you for uncertainties while allowing you to pursue opportunities. To build true financial resilience, you need to combine practical financial strategies with ethical principles, ensuring that your wealth not only benefits you but also aligns with your values.

CHAPTER GEM ELEMENTS

❖ **Financial Stability:** Essential for reducing stress, enabling long-term planning, and fostering personal growth.

❖ **Impact of Financial Stress:** Recognize the significant toll of financial stress on mental, emotional, and physical well-being, highlighting the need for resilience.

❖ **Ethical Financial Practices:** Building trust and achieving long-term success require honesty, integrity, and fairness in financial dealings.

❖ **Fair Trade and Wealth Distribution:** Promote equitable financial transactions to create a more resilient and just community.

❖ **Avoiding Exploitation:** Adhere to ethical principles, such as avoiding usury, to maintain economic stability and resilience.

❖ **Trust and Contentment:** Embrace a mindset of sufficiency and gratitude, understanding that true financial freedom comes from contentment, not just wealth.

❖ **Equitable Distribution:** Ensure fairness in resource allocation, as demonstrated by managing wealth equitably, which strengthens overall economic resilience.

❖ **Proactive Crisis Management:** Prepare for financial uncertainties by setting aside savings and proactively planning to handle unexpected challenges.

Chapter 11: Strength in Unity

Fostering Collective and Global Resilience

In an increasingly interconnected world, the resilience of communities and nations is as important as the resilience of individuals. Collective resilience; where communities, organizations, and even nations work together to overcome challenges; is vital for addressing global issues that no single person or group can tackle alone. This chapter explores the power of community and how the teachings of Prophet Muhammad (PBUH) provide a timeless model for fostering unity and resilience on a collective scale.

11.1 The Power of Community

Why Collective Resilience Matters

Collective resilience is the ability of a community or group to withstand, recover from, and adapt to adversity. It enhances individual resilience by providing a support network and shared resources. When people come together, they can pool their strengths, share the burden of challenges, and create solutions that benefit everyone involved.

1. **Support Networks**: One of the key benefits of collective resilience is the support networks it creates. In times of crisis, individuals who are part of a strong community can rely on each other for emotional, financial, and physical support. This interconnectedness not only eases the burden on individuals but also speeds up the recovery process for the entire community.

- o **Example**: During natural disasters, communities that are well-connected and organized are often able to respond more effectively, distributing aid and resources quickly and efficiently.

2. **Resource Sharing**: Collective resilience allows for the sharing of resources, which can be crucial in times of scarcity. Whether it's food, shelter, information, or skills, sharing resources ensures that everyone has access to what they need to survive and thrive.
    - o **Example**: In many traditional societies, communal farming and shared food stores were common practices that helped entire communities survive difficult seasons.

3. **Shared Purpose and Motivation**: A sense of shared purpose unites people, giving them the motivation to work together toward a common goal. This collective effort can lead to innovative solutions and a stronger, more cohesive community.
    - o **Example**: During the COVID-19 pandemic, communities that came together to support local businesses, care for the vulnerable, and follow health guidelines showed higher levels of resilience and recovery.

Reflection: Collective resilience enhances individual resilience by providing support networks, enabling resource sharing, and fostering a shared sense of purpose. In a globalized world, building strong, resilient communities is essential for addressing the challenges we all face.

Shared Challenges: Global Resilience in a Connected World

In today's interconnected world, the challenges we face; whether they are environmental, economic, or social; are often global in nature. Shared resilience is the concept that we must work together across borders and cultures to address these challenges effectively.

1. **Global Cooperation**: Many of the most pressing issues, such as climate change, pandemics, and economic instability, require global cooperation to solve. No single nation or community can tackle these problems alone. Collective resilience on a global scale involves collaboration between governments, organizations, and individuals worldwide.
   - **Example**: The Paris Agreement on climate change is an example of global cooperation, where countries around the world have come together to set targets for reducing greenhouse gas emissions.
2. **Interconnected Economies**: In a globalized economy, financial crises in one part of the world can quickly spread to others. Building economic resilience requires cooperation between nations, including fair trade practices, shared economic policies, and mutual support during crises.
   - **Example**: During the 2008 financial crisis, coordinated efforts by central banks and governments around the world helped stabilize the global economy.

3. **Cultural Exchange and Understanding**: Cultural exchange and understanding are key to fostering global resilience. By appreciating and learning from the diverse experiences and practices of others, we can build stronger, more adaptable societies.

   o **Example**: International educational programs and cultural exchanges help foster mutual understanding and respect, laying the groundwork for global cooperation and resilience.

Reflection: In an interconnected world, global resilience requires cooperation across borders and cultures. By working together to address shared challenges, we can build a more resilient and sustainable future for all.

11.2 The Prophet's Vision for Unity

Prophet Muhammad's life serves as a timeless blueprint for collective resilience. His ability to unite fragmented communities into a cohesive whole offers critical lessons for fostering unity and resilience in modern society.

Uniting the Arab Tribes

Before Islam, the Arab tribes were locked in endless feuds and divisions. Prophet Muhammad didn't just bring a new faith; he forged a new identity. Under his leadership, these tribes transformed into a united Muslim Ummah, finding strength in shared purpose. This unity, grounded in faith, allowed them to overcome both internal strife and external threats, demonstrating that resilience is born from collective vision and purpose.

The Farewell Pilgrimage: A Lasting Call for Unity

In his final sermon at the Farewell Pilgrimage, Prophet Muhammad (PBUH) proclaimed the equality of all believers, regardless of race or status. This declaration wasn't just a moral statement but a powerful guide for building a unified, resilient community. By centering unity and equality, he laid the groundwork for a community that could weather both external and internal challenges.

The Medina Charter: A Model for Inclusive Resilience

The Medina Charter stands as one of the earliest constitutions, designed to unite Muslims, Jews, and other tribes in a multi-faith society. Through mutual protection and shared responsibility, the Prophet created a resilient, diverse community that maintained harmony even under pressure. His approach teaches us that lasting resilience isn't about erasing differences but embracing them while working toward common goals.

Strength in Diplomacy

Prophet Muhammad's vision for unity extended globally. He reached out to world leaders through letters, offering peaceful relations and cooperation. His emphasis on diplomacy and communication demonstrates that resilience on a global scale requires both strength and tact.

In each of these stories, the Prophet's leadership exemplifies how fostering unity; whether within the Muslim community or across religious and cultural lines; creates a resilient, enduring social fabric capable of weathering the storms of history.

Prophet Muhammad's vision for global peace and unity provides a model for building resilience on a global scale. By promoting principles of justice, equality, and brotherhood, we can create a more resilient and peaceful world.

Key Takeaways

- **Collective resilience:** Collective resilience enhances individual resilience by providing support networks, enabling resource sharing, and fostering a shared sense of purpose.
- **Globalization:** In a globalized world, building strong, resilient communities and fostering global cooperation are essential for addressing shared challenges.
- **Sharing responsibilities:** The Medina Charter and the Prophet's leadership offer powerful examples of how unity and shared responsibility can create resilient communities.
- **Global peace:** Prophet Muhammad's vision for global peace, rooted in principles of justice, equality, and brotherhood, provides a timeless model for fostering resilience on a global scale.
- **Unified Purpose:** The Prophet's unification of the Arab tribes under Islam demonstrates the power of a shared purpose in fostering resilience. Unity in diversity strengthens communities and allows them to face challenges together.

- **Global Brotherhood:** The Prophet's emphasis on equality and brotherhood during his Farewell Pilgrimage teaches that collective resilience is built on the principles of justice and inclusivity. A global community that values equality is better equipped to support each other in times of crisis.

- **Inclusive Policies:** The Prophet's efforts to include and protect non-Muslim communities highlight the importance of inclusivity in building resilient societies. Ensuring that all members of society feel valued and protected fosters collective strength and harmony.

- **Trust and Support**: The act of consultation builds trust within the community and ensures psychological stability, as individuals feel supported and heard. This sense of emotional security contributes to the community's overall resilience.

Reflection: Strength lies in unity and inclusivity. Foster a sense of shared purpose, promote equality, and build inclusive communities to enhance collective and global resilience.

11.3 Fostering Resilience in Your Community

Building Inclusive Communities

Resilience isn't just an individual pursuit; it's a collective endeavor. Imagine a community where every voice is heard, where diversity isn't just tolerated but celebrated. That's the kind of inclusive community that can weather any storm. To build such a community, start by creating spaces where everyone feels welcome; where differences in background, opinion, and experience are not just accepted but valued. This requires active listening, empathy, and a commitment to fostering connections between people who might not otherwise cross paths.

Inclusion isn't just a moral obligation; it's a practical necessity. Diverse perspectives lead to innovative solutions, making the community stronger and more resilient. So, whether it's through community events, local organizations, or even online groups, make a concerted effort to include everyone. Encourage participation, and actively seek out voices that might otherwise go unheard.

Engaging in Collective Action

We live in a world where global challenges; from climate change to social inequality; affect us all. The magnitude of these problems can make individual efforts seem insignificant, but when we come together, our collective action can drive real change. The Prophet Muhammad's unification of the tribes under the Medina Charter is a prime example of the power of collective action. He understood that unity, even among diverse groups, was the key to overcoming existential threats.

Today, engaging in collective action might mean participating in global movements, supporting local initiatives, or even just educating yourself and others about the issues that matter. Remember, resilience is not just about surviving; it's about thriving together. When we join forces, our combined strength can tackle challenges that seem insurmountable alone.

Ethical Leadership

Leadership isn't just about being in charge; it's about being responsible. Ethical leadership is about recognizing that your actions ripple out into the world, affecting not just your immediate circle but the global community. The Prophet Muhammad's leadership during the establishment of the Ummah is a timeless example. His emphasis on justice, equality, and mutual support laid the foundation for a resilient community that has endured for centuries.

In today's interconnected world, ethical leadership means taking global responsibility seriously. Whether you're leading a team at work, a community group, or just your own family, your actions can contribute to building collective resilience. Lead with integrity, prioritize the well-being of others, and always consider the long-term impact of your decisions.

11.4 Reflect and Apply

Personal Reflection

Take a moment to reflect on your role in your community. Are you contributing to its resilience, or are you passively observing from the sidelines? Consider how you engage with others, how you respond to challenges, and how inclusive your approach is. True resilience comes from the strength of our connections and our willingness to support one another.

Action Steps

1. **Create Inclusive Spaces:** Start small; invite someone new to a community event, or initiate a

conversation with someone whose perspective you don't usually hear.

2. **Join or Start a Collective Effort:** Find a cause that resonates with you and get involved. Whether it's a local environmental initiative or a global social justice movement, your participation matters.

3. **Practice Ethical Leadership:** In your daily life, lead by example. Make decisions that reflect your values and consider how they impact the broader community.

By fostering resilience in your community, you're not just building a stronger neighborhood; you're contributing to a more resilient world.

CHAPTER GEM ELEMENTS

* **Collective Resilience:** Build strength through shared purpose, resource pooling, and unified support networks.

* **Global Cooperation:** Foster resilience by uniting communities to address shared global challenges.

* **Shared Responsibility:** Create lasting resilience by embracing collective accountability within communities.

* **Unified Purpose:** Harness the power of a shared vision to strengthen and unify diverse groups.

* **Global Brotherhood:** Promote equality and inclusivity for a global community that thrives in times of crisis.

* **Inclusive Policies:** Protect and empower all members of society to cultivate a resilient, harmonious collective.

* **Trust and Consultation:** Build trust and emotional security through inclusive decision-making and support.

Chapter 12: Stories of Strength

Learning from Real-Life Resilience

In this chapter, we dive into powerful stories from the life of Prophet Muhammad, highlighting moments of profound resilience. From overcoming personal loss in his early years to leading his followers through the Hijra and displaying forgiveness after battles, these stories offer timeless lessons. Through these narratives, you'll uncover key insights on perseverance, compassion, and moral strength; tools that are just as vital today as they were then. Finally, you'll be guided to apply these lessons in crafting your own resilience journey.

12.1 Inspirational Stories from the Prophet's Life

Overcoming Adversity

Resilience is often forged in the crucible of adversity, and there is perhaps no greater example of this than the life of Prophet Muhammad. From his early years, the Prophet faced profound challenges. Orphaned at a young age, losing both his parents before he was even six years old, he was left to navigate a world that seemed stacked against him. Yet, these early experiences of loss and vulnerability did not break him; instead, they shaped his extraordinary character, instilling in him the strength and compassion that would later define his prophetic mission.

The Prophet's early life teaches us that resilience is not the absence of pain, but the ability to find purpose and strength through it. These experiences laid the foundation for his deep empathy and understanding of human suffering, traits that would become central to his leadership and message.

The Support of Khadijah: The Role of Women in Building Islam

One of the most powerful examples of resilience in the Prophet's life is the role of Khadijah, his first wife. After the first revelation, the Prophet Muhammad (PBUH) was deeply shaken, overwhelmed by the magnitude of the message he had received. In this moment of profound uncertainty, it was Khadijah who provided the support and reassurance he needed to embrace his prophetic mission.

Khadijah's unwavering belief in her husband's mission and her emotional and psychological support were vital. She was his confidante, his advisor, and his source of strength. Her role highlights the crucial importance of strong personal connections in building resilience. It wasn't just the Prophet's inner strength that allowed him to persevere; it was also the support of those closest to him, particularly Khadijah, that enabled him to fulfill his mission. This story underscores the importance of having a strong support system, reminding us that resilience is often a collective effort.

The Perseverance of Abu Talib

Abu Talib, the Prophet's uncle, is a testament to the power of perseverance in the face of societal pressure. Despite not embracing Islam himself, his loyalty and unwavering support for his nephew were critical to the survival of the early Muslim community. The Quraysh relentlessly pressured him to abandon Muhammad, yet Abu Talib's resilience allowed him to shield the Prophet from harm, ensuring that the Islamic message continued to spread. His perseverance wasn't driven by personal gain or belief in the religion but by a deep sense of duty and familial loyalty. Source: Fada'il al-A'mal

This illustrates that resilience is not always about personal conviction in a cause but can come from a commitment to protect those we care for, even in the face of overwhelming odds.

The Loyalty of Abu Bakr: The Power of Friendship

True resilience is often bolstered by the loyalty and support of close friends, and the story of Abu Bakr during the Hijra (migration to Medina) is a testament to this. When the Prophet and Abu Bakr were hiding in the cave of Thawr, pursued by their enemies, it was Abu Bakr's steadfast loyalty and companionship that provided the Prophet with much-needed reassurance.

Abu Bakr's loyalty was not just a matter of physical presence; it was his emotional support and unwavering faith that helped the Prophet remain resilient in the face of grave danger. This story illustrates the critical role that deep, trusting relationships play in bolstering resilience. In times of crisis, it is often the loyalty and support of friends that help us find the strength to carry on.

The Patience of the Family of Yasir: Enduring Faith

The story of the family of Yasir is a poignant example of resilience in the face of unimaginable suffering. As early converts to Islam, Yasir, his wife Sumayyah, and their son Ammar faced brutal persecution in Mecca. Despite the torture they endured, Yasir and Sumayyah remained steadfast in their faith, ultimately becoming the first martyrs in Islam.

The Prophet consoled them by promising paradise, reinforcing the idea that resilience is deeply tied to enduring faith and conviction. The story of Yasir's family became a symbol of strength for the early Muslim community, showing that even in the face of death, resilience is found in holding steadfast to one's beliefs.

The Perseverance of Bilal ibn Rabah: Unwavering Conviction

Bilal ibn Rabah, an Ethiopian slave, faced excruciating torture for his belief in Islam. Despite the physical and emotional pain inflicted upon him, Bilal remained resolute, continuously proclaiming "Ahad, Ahad" (God is One). His story is a powerful testament to the resilience that comes from unwavering faith and conviction.

Bilal's perseverance under such extreme circumstances serves as an enduring example of how inner strength can transcend physical suffering. His story reminds us that true resilience often involves enduring hardship with an unshakable belief in something greater than oneself.

The Determination of Umm Salamah: The Strength of Patience

Umm Salamah, one of the Prophet's wives, faced the heart-wrenching challenge of being separated from her husband and child for an entire year due to the persecution they faced in Mecca. Despite the emotional pain of separation, Umm Salamah remained determined to reunite with her family. Her resilience in the face of such hardship made her a powerful example of inner strength and perseverance.

Umm Salamah's story teaches us that resilience is not just about enduring suffering; it's about maintaining hope and determination even when the odds seem insurmountable. Her unwavering patience and resolve serve as a reminder that true strength often lies in the ability to persist through the most challenging of circumstances.

The Endurance of the Muslims in Abyssinian Exile

When the oppression in Mecca reached unbearable levels, a group of Muslims, led by Ja'far ibn Abi Talib, sought refuge in Abyssinia (modern-day Ethiopia). They were far from their homeland, surrounded by unfamiliar people and customs, yet they endured. Their endurance was not simply about survival; it was about maintaining their faith, unity, and identity despite being in exile. Their resilience in this foreign land became a beacon of hope, allowing Islam to survive during a time when it was threatened by the overwhelming powers in Mecca. The Abyssinian Muslims remind us that sometimes resilience is about enduring the unknown and finding strength in unity, even when everything familiar is stripped away. Source: Al-Sirah al-Nabawiyyah

The Hijra: A Testament to Collective Resilience

The Hijra, the migration from Mecca to Medina, is one of the most significant events in Islamic history. It was a journey fraught with danger, requiring immense physical, emotional, and spiritual resilience. The Prophet's leadership during the Hijra not only exemplified his personal resilience but also the collective resilience of the early Muslim community.

The Hijra was not just a physical migration; it was a transformative event that solidified the Muslim community's identity and unity. The challenges faced during this journey and the resilience displayed by the Prophet and his followers became a defining moment in the establishment of Islam. The Hijra teaches us that resilience is often a collective effort, requiring the strength and unity of an entire community.

Forgiveness and Mercy: The Prophet's Strength in Compassion

One of the most profound aspects of the Prophet Muhammad's resilience was his ability to forgive, even in the face of intense adversity. This is perhaps most clearly demonstrated during the Conquest of Mecca, where the Prophet chose to forgive those who had persecuted him and his followers, rather than seek revenge.

This act of forgiveness was not a sign of weakness but a testament to his inner strength and moral resilience. It demonstrated that true resilience is not just about enduring hardship but also about rising above it with compassion and mercy. The Prophet's ability to forgive, even in the most trying circumstances, highlights the power of compassion as a cornerstone of resilience.

And here is my favorite;

The story of Prophet Muhammad pawning his shield to a Jewish man is a well-known and authentic narrative, found in Sahih al-Bukhari. Toward the end of his life, despite being the leader of a growing and powerful Muslim state, the Prophet Muhammad chose to live a simple life, often experiencing financial hardships.

In one instance, the Prophet needed to secure food for his household, and since he had no money, he pawned his shield with a Jewish man in exchange for some barley. This shield, an important piece of his armor, symbolized both his role as a leader and protector of the Muslim community.

This story showcases multiple lessons, including:

- **Humility:** Despite his position, the Prophet did not hesitate to engage in everyday transactions and sought assistance when needed.

- **Trust in Non-Muslims:** The Prophet's interaction with a Jewish man shows the mutual respect and trust he extended to people of different faiths, emphasizing coexistence and cooperation.

- **Simple Lifestyle:** Even when he had the means to demand or receive more, the Prophet maintained a humble lifestyle, choosing to rely on his own efforts rather than extravagant favors.

This episode of pawning his shield a masterpiece of practical resilience, where the Prophet, instead of seeing his need as a setback, used available resources wisely. It's a reflection of moral, social, and psychological resilience in how he dealt with everyday challenges in a balanced, dignified way.

"I know; it is a shocker; this is in his last days.

I cannot pass this story without asking a question; Why did he pawn his shield with a Jewish man instead of seeking help from his wealthy companions? And believe me, there were many rich companions at that time who would have gladly given him anything he asked for.

You can find my thoughts on that in the final thoughts chapter."

These stories from the Prophet's life and his companions are not just historical anecdotes; they are timeless lessons in resilience, offering us guidance on how to navigate the challenges of our own lives with strength, patience, and compassion.

12.2 Key Lessons for Modern Resilience

Perseverance: The Prophet Muhammad's life is a rich tapestry of perseverance in the face of adversity. Whether it was enduring the loss of loved ones, facing persecution, or leading his community through times of crisis, the Prophet's resilience was rooted in his unwavering commitment to his mission. For us, the lesson is clear: perseverance is key to resilience. It's not about avoiding challenges but about facing them head-on with determination and faith.

Compassion as Strength: The Prophet's life also teaches us that compassion is not a weakness but a profound source of strength. Whether through his acts of forgiveness or his deep empathy for those who suffered, the Prophet showed that resilience is deeply intertwined with the ability to care for others. In a world that often values toughness and self-reliance, the Prophet's example reminds us that true resilience comes from a place of compassion and understanding.

Resilience through Relationships: Strong, supportive relationships are a cornerstone of resilience. Whether it's the support of a spouse, the loyalty of a friend, or the determination of a loved one, these connections provide the emotional strength needed to overcome adversity.

Resilience through Faith: Unwavering faith, as demonstrated by figures like Bilal ibn Rabah and the family of Yasir, is a profound source of resilience. Belief in a higher purpose can sustain individuals through even the most severe trials.

Resilience through Leadership: The Prophet Muhammad's ability to lead with mercy, unify his followers, and make strategic decisions during crises exemplifies how resilience in leadership can shape the course of history.

Resilience through Forgiveness: The ability to forgive, even when wronged, is a powerful form of resilience. It requires immense inner strength and the capacity to transcend personal grievances for the greater good.

Resilience through Sacrifice: The Hijra illustrates that resilience often requires sacrifice and the courage to undertake difficult journeys, both literal and metaphorical, for the sake of a higher purpose.

Courage in Adversity: Abu Talib's protection of the Prophet, despite facing immense pressure, teaches that resilience often requires courage and standing firm in your convictions, even when it's difficult.

Endurance in Exile: The resilience of the Muslims in Abyssinia under Ja'far ibn Abi Talib's leadership shows that even in exile, maintaining faith and unity can help a community survive and thrive. Resilience is about enduring hardships with dignity and hope.

Reflection: Real-life resilience is built on strong partnerships, courage in adversity, and endurance in the face of challenges. Draw inspiration from these stories of strength to build your own resilience.

12.3 Crafting Your Own Resilience Story

Learning from the Past: Drawing Inspiration from the Prophet's Life and his companions.

The life of Prophet Muhammad (PBUH) is a wellspring of inspiration for those seeking to build their resilience. His experiences, marked by profound challenges and remarkable perseverance, serve as timeless lessons in how to navigate adversity with grace and strength. But these stories are not just historical tales; they are blueprints for how we can face our own challenges today.

The Prophet's ability to rise above personal loss, lead a persecuted community, and maintain his commitment to compassion and forgiveness in the face of hostility offers us a powerful framework. We can look at his life and see the embodiment of resilience, a model for how to endure and thrive even when the world seems most against us. The key is to take these lessons and apply them to our own lives, using the Prophet's life as a mirror to reflect on our own journeys.

By examining how the Prophet overcame the death of his parents, the support he received from Khadijah, the loyalty of Abu Bakr, the perseverance of Bilal, and the patience of the family of Yasir, we can glean insights into how to handle our own struggles. These stories encourage us to ask ourselves:

- How can we channel such strength in our moments of hardship?
- What can we learn from these examples to help us face our own trials with resilience and grace?

Your Resilience Narrative: Crafting Your Own Story of Strength

Just as the Prophet's life was a series of trials that he met with resilience, each of us has our own story to tell; a narrative shaped by the challenges we've faced and the ways we've overcome them. Crafting your own resilience story is not just an exercise in reflection; it's a powerful tool for personal growth and empowerment.

Start by looking at your life through the lens of resilience. Identify the moments where you faced significant challenges. These could be personal losses, professional setbacks, health issues, or any other obstacles that tested your strength.

- How did you respond?
- What strategies did you use to cope, and how did these experiences shape who you are today?

Next, think about the lessons you've learned from these experiences. Did you develop a greater sense of patience? Did you discover inner reserves of strength that you didn't know you had? Perhaps you found solace in relationships, much like the Prophet did with Khadijah and Abu Bakr, or maybe your faith played a crucial role in helping you persevere. These insights are the foundation of your resilience narrative.

Once you've identified these key moments and lessons, consider how you can share your story with others. Your resilience narrative can serve as a source of inspiration and guidance for those around you, just as the stories from the Prophet's life continue to inspire and guide us. Whether through writing, speaking, or simply living by example, sharing your resilience story can help others see that they too have the strength to overcome their challenges.

Recognize Your Strengths: What inner strengths did you draw upon during these challenges? Were you patient, determined, or did you rely on the support of others? Identify the qualities that helped you persevere.

Link to Values: How did your core values guide your actions? Like the Prophet, were you driven by a sense of duty, justice, or faith? Understanding the values that underpin your resilience will help you craft a narrative that's deeply personal and meaningful.

Crafting your resilience story also allows you to reframe your past in a way that highlights your growth and strengths, rather than your struggles and defeats. It's about seeing yourself not as a victim of circumstances, but as a resilient individual who has the power to overcome adversity and thrive. This shift in perspective is crucial for building self-confidence and resilience moving forward.

12.4 Reflect and Apply

Personal Reflection

To truly integrate these lessons into your life, reflect on how the Prophet's stories resonate with your own experiences. Perhaps you see a parallel between your challenges and those faced by the Prophet or his companions. Identify those connections and consider how their examples can guide your future actions.

- **Which Story Resonates Most?** Is there a particular story from the Prophet's life that speaks to you? Reflect on why this story resonates and how you can draw strength from it in your current life.
- **Your Current Challenges**: Consider the challenges you are facing right now. How can the lessons of perseverance, loyalty, and faith be applied to your situation?

Action Steps

To ensure that the lessons from the Prophet's life are not just philosophical musings but actionable strategies, here are practical steps for integrating these teachings into your resilience journey:

1. **Daily Reflection**: Set aside time each day to reflect on your resilience journey. This could be through journaling or meditation. Use this time to connect your experiences with the stories you've learned.
2. **Strengthen Relationships**: Like the Prophet, lean on your support network. Strengthen your

relationships with those who uplift and support you, as these bonds will be crucial in times of adversity.

3. **Commit to Your Values**: Reaffirm your commitment to the values that guide you. Whether it's honesty, compassion, or faith, let these principles be the foundation of your resilience.

4. **Share Your Story**: Don't keep your resilience narrative to yourself. Share it with others, as storytelling is a powerful way to inspire and build collective resilience. Your story might be the strength someone else needs to overcome their own challenges.

By drawing from the profound lessons in the Prophet Muhammad's life and applying them to your own, you are not only crafting a personal resilience story but also building a life grounded in faith, values, and enduring strength.

CHAPTER GEM ELEMENTS

- ❖ **Perseverance in Adversity:** True resilience is about facing challenges with unwavering determination, not avoiding them. Perseverance, rooted in faith and purpose, is the foundation of inner strength.
- ❖ **Compassion Leadership Through Resilience:** Leadership marked by mercy, compassion, unity, and strategic decision-making during crises highlights how resilient leaders shape the future.
- ❖ **Supportive Relationships:** Strong, supportive relationships provide emotional strength, helping us navigate hardships with greater resilience.
- ❖ **Faith as a Source of Strength:** Belief in a higher purpose, as demonstrated in stories of faith, sustains individuals through even the most severe challenges.
- ❖ **Forgiveness as Inner Strength:** The ability to forgive, even when wronged, requires immense inner resilience and contributes to greater emotional freedom and strength.
- ❖ **Sacrifice for Higher Purpose:** Resilience often requires sacrifice, as seen in the willingness to undertake difficult journeys for the sake of a higher goal.
- ❖ **Courage in Adversity:** Standing firm in your convictions, even when faced with immense pressure, is a hallmark of resilience.

❖ **Endurance in Exile:** Resilience is not just about survival but thriving in adversity. Maintaining faith and unity through hardship fosters lasting endurance.

Chapter 13: Future-Proofing Your Resilience

Preparing for Tomorrow's Challenges

This chapter explores the evolving landscape of resilience in the face of emerging global challenges. From technological disruptions to environmental crises, we'll examine how resilience must adapt. The MLRM, enriched by timeless lessons from Prophet Muhammad's life, offers a powerful framework to meet these future uncertainties. By integrating flexibility, adaptability, and continuous learning, you'll be empowered to build lasting resilience that endures. Lastly, you'll reflect on your readiness for future challenges and take actionable steps toward a resilient, future-proof life.

13.1 Adapting to Emerging Challenges: The Future of Resilience

As the world evolves, so too must our understanding of resilience. The challenges of tomorrow will be shaped by forces we are just beginning to understand: rapid technological advancements, climate change, and the lingering effects of global pandemics. The concept of resilience must therefore expand, becoming as dynamic and adaptive as the world we inhabit.

To understand Prophet Muhammad (PBUH) Future-Proofing Your Resilience; let us dig deeper in some of his remarkable stories;

The Strategic Alliances Formed Before the Conquest of Mecca

Before the monumental conquest of Mecca, Prophet Muhammad (PBUH) demonstrated remarkable foresight by carefully forging alliances with key tribes surrounding the city. This wasn't a spur-of-the-moment decision but part of a meticulously crafted long-term strategy. By securing these alliances, he ensured the security of the Muslim community and paved the way for a peaceful transition of power. The Prophet's ability to see beyond the present moment, to anticipate future challenges, and to secure the necessary relationships speaks volumes about the importance of strategic foresight in resilience. In today's world, building strong, strategic alliances; whether personal, professional, or communal; remains a crucial element in navigating future uncertainties with confidence and strength. Source: "Fada'il al-A'mal"

The Establishment of Islamic Education

Prophet Muhammad's commitment to education laid the foundation for future generations to thrive, both in faith and in life. By establishing the Suffah; a dedicated school attached to the mosque in Medina; he ensured that learning was deeply integrated into the community's fabric. This wasn't just about transmitting religious knowledge; it was about empowering individuals to think, reflect, and grow resilient in the face of future challenges. Education became the bedrock of resilience, creating a community prepared to face whatever came next. In modern terms, this reflects the necessity of continuous learning and the ability to adapt through knowledge; tools that are vital for long-term resilience and success. Source: "Kitab al-Samarkandiyya"

The Instructions for Preparing for the Day of Judgment

Prophet Muhammad (PBUH) often reminded his followers of the ultimate challenge; the Day of Judgment; encouraging them to live lives filled with integrity, accountability, and a sense of purpose. This wasn't just about spiritual preparation; it was about cultivating a mindset that understood life as part of a greater continuum. This constant awareness of an inevitable future kept the community focused on living meaningfully in the present. In today's terms, this reflects the value of always thinking ahead, preparing for the future by living with intent and foresight. Whether it's the practical challenges of tomorrow or the philosophical preparation for eternity, this mindset fosters resilience that transcends the immediate moment. Source: "Dalail al-Khayrat"

With the same strategies, let us talk about the pervasive influence of technology. With AI, biotechnology, and digital networks reshaping our reality, resilience now includes the ability to navigate the complexities these innovations bring. Whether it's maintaining mental health in an increasingly virtual world or developing the skills to pivot in a tech-driven job market, our ability to adapt will be tested like never before.

The Role of Technology

Emerging technologies hold both the potential to bolster our resilience and to challenge it. On one hand, they offer tools for crisis management, from advanced predictive models for disaster preparedness to global communication networks that keep us connected. On the other, they present new risks; cybersecurity threats, digital divides, and the erosion of privacy.

For instance, consider the strategic planning for the Battle of Tabuk. The Prophet Muhammad's meticulous preparation for a potential conflict that never materialized exemplifies how we must approach future challenges. It wasn't about reacting to a crisis but anticipating it, gathering resources, and building alliances long before the threat could materialize. Similarly, in today's world, resilience demands that we prepare for technological disruptions and environmental changes before they fully emerge.

13.2 The Timelessness of MLRM

A Modern Application of Ancient Wisdom

The MLRM, inspired by the life of the Prophet Muhammad, is not just a relic of the past; it's a blueprint for navigating the future. This model, with its emphasis on moral, spiritual, emotional, and social resilience, equips us to face challenges that transcend time.

Consider the Prophet's long-term vision in drafting the Medina Constitution. This document wasn't just about resolving immediate conflicts but about laying a foundation for enduring governance, justice, and coexistence. It was an act of systemic resilience, ensuring that the community could withstand not just the challenges of the present, but those of the future as well. In a modern context, this teaches us the importance of creating systems; whether in our personal lives or in society; that are resilient to change and adaptable to new realities.

Building Future-Ready Resilience

To build resilience that withstands the uncertainties of tomorrow, we must look to strategies that are as forward-thinking as they are grounded in time-tested principles. Here are some key strategies we've extracted from the Prophet's wisdom to tackle the challenges he encountered:

- **Anticipating Future Threats:** The Prophet's careful planning for the *Hijra* from Mecca to Medina was a blueprint for future readiness. By meticulously strategizing the route, timing, and contingencies, he demonstrated the importance of not just reacting to immediate challenges but anticipating and preparing for what lies ahead. His pre-agreement with the Madina tribes, securing a safe place before venturing into the unknown, a lesson learned from Taif, was a masterclass for generations. In today's world, building resilience requires us to foresee potential disruptions; whether technological, environmental, or societal; and take steps to mitigate them before they occur.

- **Creating Resilient Communities:** The Prophet's unification of the *Muhajirun* (migrants) and *Ansar* (helpers) in Medina teaches us how to build systems that foster collaboration and unity. By forging bonds based on shared values, he ensured that the community would remain strong and adaptable to change. For modern organizations and communities, fostering inclusivity and shared responsibility is key to enduring and thriving in the face of future challenges.

- **Long-Term Vision:** The Prophet's foresight in envisioning Islam's expansion beyond the Arabian Peninsula, even while facing immediate opposition, reflects the importance of long-term thinking. Building future-ready resilience means taking actions today; whether in sustainable practices, technological innovation, or leadership development; that will pay dividends for future generations. Visionaries don't just focus on short-term gains; they lay the groundwork for a lasting legacy.

- **Building Strategic Alliances:** The Prophet's peace treaty with the Christian tribes of Najran highlights the value of forming strategic partnerships. He recognized that strong alliances would protect the Muslim community from future threats and foster mutual growth. In a rapidly evolving world, securing alliances across industries, cultures, and nations ensures we are better prepared to navigate future uncertainties and challenges.

- **Empowering Through Education:** The Prophet's focus on literacy and education, such as teaching captives to read after the Battle of Badr, reflects his belief in the power of knowledge to build future resilience. Educating and empowering people with skills and knowledge ensures that societies are equipped to handle future complexities. In our modern context, continuous learning and skill development are essential to staying future-ready in a world of constant change.

- **Strengthening Spiritual Resilience:** The *Isra and Mi'raj*; the Prophet's spiritual journey during a period of intense hardship; illustrates the power of faith to sustain resilience. In an uncertain future, having a strong sense of purpose and spiritual grounding can help individuals and organizations weather the most profound challenges, ensuring that resilience is not just physical or material but deeply rooted in meaning.

- **Adapting to Changing Circumstances:** The Prophet's decision during the Treaty of *Hudaybiyyah* to delay entering Mecca reflects his adaptive leadership. Instead of insisting on immediate success, he prioritized long-term peace, understanding that adaptability is critical for future success. In building future-ready resilience, the ability to pivot and adjust strategies in response to changing environments is essential for sustained growth and stability.

- **Proactive Infrastructure Planning:** The Prophet's establishment of the first mosque in Quba before his arrival in Medina is an example of proactive preparation for the future. Laying down physical and institutional structures early ensures that a community or organization can grow and thrive even in the face of uncertainty. Modern resilience-building involves planning infrastructures; be they technological, organizational, or social; that will support future growth and stability.

- **Inclusive Leadership for a Resilient Future:** The Prophet's role in resolving the dispute over the placement of the Black Stone in Mecca is a lesson in inclusive leadership. By involving all parties and fostering collaboration, he prevented conflict and built a stronger, more unified community. Future-ready resilience requires leaders to be inclusive, adaptable, and able to bring diverse perspectives together to solve complex problems.

- **Sustaining Vision Beyond the Present:** The Prophet's *Farewell Sermon* at the final pilgrimage laid out a clear vision for the Muslim community's future, ensuring that his teachings would continue to guide generations to come. Building future-ready resilience means ensuring that your actions today are not just for immediate survival but are part of a broader, sustainable vision that will empower future generations to thrive.

Future-proof your resilience by building strategic alliances, investing in education, and preparing for life's ultimate challenges. A forward-thinking approach ensures that you are ready to face whatever comes your way. By integrating these timeless principles into our modern lives, we can build resilience that is not just reactive but future-proof, ready to face whatever challenges the world may bring.

13.3 Taking Ownership of Your Resilience

Proactively Building Resilience with MLRM

Resilience isn't something you stumble upon in a moment of crisis; it's something you build, brick by brick, long before the storm hits. The MLRM offers a comprehensive framework for doing just that, encompassing moral, spiritual, emotional, and social resilience. But to truly empower your resilience, you must take ownership of it.

Taking ownership means being proactive rather than reactive. It's about recognizing that you have the tools and the agency to fortify yourself against the challenges that lie ahead. Just as the Prophet Muhammad (PBUH) meticulously prepared for the Battle of Tabuk, gathering resources and forging alliances, you too must prepare for the uncertainties of the future. This preparation isn't just about survival; it's about thriving in the face of adversity.

- Start by assessing each pillar of the MLRM in your life.
- Are you grounded in your moral and ethical principles?
- Do you nurture your spiritual health regularly?
- Are you emotionally and psychologically prepared to handle stress and change?

- How strong is your social and community network?

And so, on

By identifying your strengths and weaknesses in each area, you can begin to build a resilience plan that is tailored to your unique needs and circumstances.

Planning for the Future

Building long-term resilience requires more than just a strong foundation; it requires a clear vision of the future. This is where goal-setting and adaptability come into play. The Prophet's long-term vision in the drafting of the Medina Constitution is a perfect example of planning with foresight. He didn't just address the needs of his community in the present but laid down a blueprint for future generations, ensuring that the community could withstand and adapt to future challenges.

When planning for your own future, start by setting clear, actionable goals. These should be aligned with the pillars of the MLRM, ensuring that you're building resilience across all areas of your life. For example, you might set a goal to strengthen your social network by participating in community activities or to enhance your emotional resilience by practicing mindfulness and stress management techniques.

Adaptability is equally crucial. The world is constantly changing, and so too must your resilience strategies. Just as the Prophet's community had to adapt to new realities after the drafting of the Medina Constitution, you must be prepared to revise your goals and strategies as circumstances evolve. This doesn't mean abandoning your plan at the first sign of trouble; it means being flexible enough to adjust your course while keeping your long-term vision intact.

13.4 Reflect and Apply

Personal Reflection

To truly future-proof your resilience, you need to take a hard look at where you stand today. Are you prepared for the challenges that tomorrow might bring? Reflect on the stories and lessons drawn from the life of the Prophet Muhammad, and compare them to your own life experiences. Have you built a strong moral foundation? Are you nurturing your spiritual and emotional well-being? How robust is your social support network?

This reflection isn't just about identifying gaps; it's about recognizing your strengths as well. The journey of resilience is as much about acknowledging what you've already built as it is about planning for what's to come. Take pride in the resilience you've already developed, and use it as a foundation to build upon as you prepare for the future.

Action Steps for Future-Proofing Resilience

1. **Set Long-Term Goals**: Establish clear, actionable goals that align with the pillars of the MLRM. These should be specific, measurable, achievable, relevant, and time-bound (SMART). For example, if you want to strengthen your emotional resilience, you might set a goal to practice mindfulness meditation for 10 minutes every day.

2. **Create a Resilience Plan**: Develop a comprehensive resilience plan that addresses each area of the MLRM. This plan should include strategies for maintaining moral and ethical integrity, nurturing your spiritual health, managing stress and emotions, and building strong social connections.

3. **Regularly Reassess and Adapt**: Just as the Prophet's community adapted to new challenges after the drafting of the Medina Constitution, you should regularly reassess your resilience plan and be prepared to make adjustments as needed. Life is unpredictable, and your resilience plan should be flexible enough to adapt to changing circumstances.

4. **Build a Support Network**: Resilience is not a solo endeavor. Strengthen your social network by engaging with your community, seeking out like-minded individuals, and building relationships based on trust and mutual support. The stronger your network, the more resilient you will be in the face of future challenges.

5. **Invest in Continuous Learning**: The world is constantly changing, and so should your knowledge and skills. Commit to lifelong learning, whether it's through formal education, self-study, or learning from others in your community. The more knowledge and skills you have, the better equipped you'll be to adapt to future challenges.

Reflection:

- **Proactive Ownership**: Empower your resilience by taking proactive ownership of your life, using the MLRM as a comprehensive guide.

- **Future-Oriented Planning**: Just as the Prophet Muhammad (PBUH) planned for long-term community resilience, you should set clear, actionable goals and be adaptable in your approach to building resilience.

- **Regular Reflection and Adaptation**: Continuously assess your readiness for future challenges and adapt your resilience strategies as needed to ensure you remain strong and capable, no matter what the future holds.

By integrating these principles into your daily life, you can build a resilience that is not only strong enough to withstand the challenges of today but flexible and forward-thinking enough to thrive in the uncertainties of tomorrow.

CHAPTER GEM ELEMENTS

- ❖ **Anticipating Future Threats:** Proactively identify potential disruptions and develop strategies to mitigate them before they arise.
- ❖ **Building Strategic Alliances:** Forge strong partnerships across industries and cultures to enhance resilience in navigating uncertainties.
- ❖ **Empowering Through Education:** Invest in continuous learning and skill development to prepare individuals and societies for future complexities.
- ❖ **Proactive Infrastructure Planning:** Establish physical, technological, and organizational structures early to support future growth.
- ❖ **Inclusive Leadership:** Engage diverse perspectives to foster collaboration and resolve conflicts, thereby strengthening future-ready resilience.
- ❖ **Long-Term Vision in Governance and Leadership:** Develop a sustainable, long-term vision that empowers future generations to thrive and grow.

Epilogue

Why did I write this book? It's simple; I'm tired. Tired of seeing millions of academic articles and research papers churned out, with endless hours poured into crafting them, only for them to gather dust on library shelves or sit in the storage basements of universities. You pour your soul into your work, only to watch it vanish into academic obscurity. And when you try to get your work published in academic journals, you face reviewers who think they're doing you a favor by shifting your ideas, reshaping them into something you barely recognize. It's as if the original spirit gets diluted, lost in the maze of intellectual gatekeeping.

That's why this book had to be different. My mission? To make these important discussions accessible, to strip away the layers of elitism and jargon, while still maintaining the depth and professionalism that serious readers deserve. I wanted to bridge that gap; between the academic world and the general public; without dumbing anything down. I wanted to bring people into the conversation, to offer them insights without forcing them through frustrating journal reviews or scholarly paths they never signed up for.

I've achieved this by trying to maintain language that is both sharp and simple. No fluff, no goofiness; just clean, straightforward content. I've also embraced systems thinking, not only because it's modern and relatable but because it resonates with how people naturally process the complexities of life. If you noticed, I've gradually presented it throughout the chapters, beginning with less structured sections and progressing to more structured chapters with key takeaways at the end. I'm simply aiming to lessen the academic tone of the theory and make it less enticing. This approach is meant to be digestible, offering everyone a way in, regardless of their background.

And yes, I've deliberately avoided the traditional referencing style. This book isn't meant to look like another academic paper; it's for everyone. Whether you're a scholar, a student, or someone who's never set foot in a university, this book is for you. It's written with respect for your intellect but without the obstacles that typically stand between you and the knowledge you deserve.

And that, my friend, is the walk-the-talk of resilience itself.

Heads up! The following section dives into academic concepts terms and theories that might ruffle some feathers. Proceed with caution!

I just need to explain what systems thinking is and how it's used to build the model. Feel free to skip ahead if this sounds like a snooze fest!

Integrating Systems Thinking and Modern Frameworks

When shaping the ideas in this book, the goal wasn't simply to recount historical stories or present religious teachings in isolation. Instead, the approach was guided by modern frameworks of resilience, particularly **Systems Thinking**; a theory that emphasizes seeing the bigger picture and understanding how different elements interact within a larger system. In a world where complexity defines almost every challenge we face, relying on isolated solutions or single events doesn't cut it. And that's where Systems Thinking becomes invaluable.

Systems Thinking essentially teaches us that everything exists within a network of interrelated components. It moves beyond linear, cause-and-effect thinking, encouraging us to look at the relationships and dynamics between various parts. By applying this to the resilience model we've constructed from the life of the Prophet Muhammad, we are better able to capture the broader impact of his leadership and strategies. Muhammad (PBUH) didn't just react to problems; he implemented solutions that worked in harmony with the social, political, and economic systems around him. His leadership was deeply interconnected with the people, the culture, and the time, allowing for an adaptive, flexible approach to resilience.

Let's break it down further:

1. Resilience as a System

At its core, resilience is not a single trait or a one-time reaction to adversity. It's a system; a network of interrelated factors that come together to create an adaptive, enduring response to challenges. In shaping the **Muhammad's Lasting Resilience Model (MLRM),** we adopted this systemic view, understanding that Prophet Muhammad's life presents a holistic resilience framework. His leadership strategies weren't isolated; they were embedded in a broader, interconnected system of moral, social, and spiritual components.

For example, his delegation of responsibilities among his companions wasn't merely an act of trust; it was a calculated move to create a decentralized leadership system that could function independently of his presence or his absence. This ensures that when one part of the system is under pressure, others can step in to support, ensuring continuity and strength. Each person had a role within the larger structure, much like how modern organizations rely on various departments, each functioning independently but interconnectedly, to thrive in challenging times.

2. Interconnectedness and Adaptation

Systems Thinking also highlights the importance of **feedback loops**; where actions create reactions, and those reactions inform future actions. Prophet Muhammad's life offers countless examples of this. Take the Constitution of Medina, for instance. It wasn't just about creating a document and moving forward; it was about constantly adapting and responding to the needs and dynamics of the diverse tribes and faith groups under its rule. This flexible governance allowed the Muslim community to evolve, reinforcing the feedback loop of stability, trust, and growth.

In modern terms, it's like refining a business strategy based on real-time data. Muhammad's leadership continuously evolved based on the outcomes of his actions and the responses of his community, demonstrating how adaptive, feedback-driven systems work. This is a hallmark of resilient organizations today; those that don't just set a course and stick to it, but constantly re-evaluate based on new challenges and information. In addition, as a leader, he fostered trust and support through the practice of consultation "Shura". This approach, built trust within the community and ensured psychological stability, as individuals felt valued and heard. This sense of emotional security significantly contributed to the community's overall resilience.

3. Integration of Modern Frameworks

In addition to Systems Thinking, we drew from contemporary resilience frameworks like **Cognitive Behavioral Therapy (CBT)** and the **GROW model** (Goal, Reality, Options, Way forward). These models emphasize self-awareness, flexibility, and a structured approach to problem-solving, which align perfectly with the way Muhammad (PBUH) navigated crises and built a robust community.

- **CBT principles** were clearly reflected in his leadership style, particularly in how he encouraged his followers to adopt healthier, more constructive thought patterns. His emphasis on faith, patience, and positive mindset (Husn al-Dhann) mirrors the cognitive restructuring techniques in CBT, where individuals challenge their limiting beliefs and replace them with empowering, action-oriented thoughts. This is resilience at a psychological level; a fundamental part of the MLRM.

- The **GROW model**, commonly used in coaching and leadership development, also echoes in Muhammad's method of leadership. He consistently helped his companions **identify goals** (spiritual and community growth), **assess reality** (recognizing the political and social challenges), **explore options** (strategizing based on feedback), and **plan a way forward** (implementing solutions like the Treaty of Hudaybiyyah or the formation of the marketplace in Medina). This systematic, forward-thinking approach reflects the essence of goal-oriented leadership that's critical in fostering organizational resilience.

4. Long-Term Vision and Sustainability

Systems Thinking pushes us to think beyond the short-term, and Muhammad's leadership exemplifies this forward-looking vision. His solutions weren't quick fixes; they were designed to build a sustainable, resilient community. Consider his approach to the Treaty of Hudaybiyyah. While it seemed like a compromise in the short-term, it ultimately paved the way for long-term peace and the eventual growth of the Muslim state. He recognized that true resilience doesn't mean winning every battle; it means making decisions today that will strengthen the entire system for the challenges of tomorrow.

Similarly, the establishment of a marketplace in Medina was more than just an economic boost; it created a system that could withstand external pressures and internal disruptions, providing long-term stability. This mirrors the **concept of antifragility** (as popularized by Nassim Nicholas Taleb), where systems grow stronger when exposed to stressors. Muhammad's strategies were not just about survival; they were about thriving through adversity.

As has been illustrated above, **Systems Thinking** served as a guiding principle to present Prophet Muhammad's life as more than just a collection of individual stories. His actions, decisions, and leadership formed a cohesive, adaptive system; one that responded to the immediate needs of the time but also prepared for future challenges. By integrating modern frameworks like CBT, the GROW model, antifragility, and more; we've developed a resilience model that's not only timeless but also applicable to modern life.

The Theory Behind MLRM

The MLRM is built on the theory that true resilience is multidimensional, requiring an integration of moral, spiritual, emotional, psychological, organizational, social, and community resilience. This theory is grounded in the belief that resilience is not just an individual trait but a collective capacity that is cultivated through interconnected systems of support, ethical practices, and spiritual grounding.

The theory behind MLRM is intricately woven into the model itself, articulated through its framework and core principles. You'll notice it aligns seamlessly with well-known resilience theories, while also introducing new dimensions to fill the gaps and build an ultimate resilience model.

Key Theoretical Foundations:

1. **Systems Theory:**
   o **Holistic Integration**: The model operates on the principle that all aspects of human experience; moral, spiritual, emotional, psychological, social, and community; are interconnected systems. These systems must be developed and maintained in harmony to build robust resilience.
2. **Social Support Theory:**
   o **Strength in Connections**: The theory emphasizes the critical role of social networks and community support in enhancing resilience. It posits that resilience

is not an isolated trait but one that is significantly strengthened through relationships and collective effort.

3. **Cognitive Behavioral Theory (CBT):**
   o **Mastering Your Emotions**: The model incorporates principles ·from CBT, particularly the idea that emotional resilience can be built through cognitive restructuring, reflection, and strategic emotional regulation.

4. **Adaptive Leadership Theory:**
   o **Leading with Resilience**: MLRM aligns with the concept of adaptive leadership, which focuses on the ability to navigate complex challenges, innovate under pressure, and lead organizations through uncertain times.

5. **Transformational Learning Theory:**
   o **Lifelong Learning**: The model advocates for continuous learning and growth, aligning with transformational learning theory, which suggests that individuals can achieve profound personal and professional development through critical reflection and active engagement with new knowledge.

6. **Moral and Ethical Theories:**
   o **Inner Strength and Ethical Resilience**: MLRM draws heavily from moral and ethical theories, particularly those rooted in religious and spiritual teachings. The model posits that moral integrity and spiritual

discipline are foundational to true resilience, providing a compass for navigating life's challenges.

7. **Organizational and Community Resilience Theories:**
   o MLRM emphasizing proactive planning, ethical leadership, and adaptive systems, which are core principles in both frameworks. It goes further by embedding spiritual, moral, and social resilience, fostering a sense of shared purpose, deeper ethical grounding, and long-term sustainability, elevating standard resilience models.

8. **Post-Traumatic Growth Theory:**
   o **Stories of Strength**: The model aligns with post-traumatic growth theory, which suggests that individuals can experience significant personal growth following adversity, particularly when supported by strong social networks and a resilient mindset.

MLRM as A Comprehensive Blueprint for Resilience

By now, you should grasp that MLRM is not only aligned with but also transcends existing resilience theories, offering a superior path for individuals, organizations, communities, and societies to thrive amidst adversity.

Core Principles of MLRM

At the heart of MLRM lies a set of core principles that serve as the foundation for building resilience:

1. **Holistic Integration**: MLRM emphasizes the interconnectedness of moral, spiritual, emotional, psychological, social, and community resilience, recognizing that true resilience is cultivated across all dimensions of life.
2. **Actionable Wisdom**: Drawing from the life of Prophet Muhammad, MLRM provides practical guidance and strategies that can be applied in real-world scenarios, making resilience not just a theoretical concept but a lived experience.
3. **Timelessness and Universality**: The principles of MLRM are rooted in universal values and timeless wisdom, ensuring their relevance across cultures, contexts, and eras.
4. **Future-Proofing**: MLRM is designed to equip individuals and communities with the tools to adapt to and thrive in the face of future uncertainties, making it a forward-looking model.

The Foundational Pillars of MLRM

Muhammad (PBUH) anchored his resilience on two foundational pillars, instilling the same in his companions and followers: unwavering belief in faith and destiny (Tawakkul and Qadr) and harnessing the transformative power of positive affirmation (Husn al-Dhann and Positive Mindset).

✓ **Belief in Faith and Destiny (Tawakkul and Qadr)**

At the heart of the MLRM lies an unwavering belief in Tawakkul and Qadr; trust in divine will and the acceptance of destiny. This principle teaches us to embrace the uncertainty of life with confidence, knowing that every event, whether joyous or painful, is part of a grand design. It's about understanding that while we have control over our actions, the outcomes are ultimately in the hands of a higher power.

This belief cultivates a profound sense of inner peace, allowing individuals to remain grounded in the face of adversity. It encourages a mindset where one becomes comfortable with discomfort, accepting challenges not as obstacles but as divinely ordained opportunities for growth. By integrating Tawakkul into our daily lives, we develop the strength to persevere, even when the road ahead seems uncertain or daunting. It's about having faith that, in the grand scheme, everything unfolds as it should, and there is wisdom in every twist and turn of our journey.

✓ **The Power of Positive Affirmation (Husn al-Dhann and Positive Mindset)**

Equally essential to the MLRM is the power of positive affirmation, rooted in the Islamic concept of Husn al-Dhann; having a good opinion of Allah and, by extension, a positive outlook on life. This principle emphasizes that our thoughts and beliefs shape our reality. By maintaining a positive mindset, we invite positive outcomes. It's the idea that after every hardship comes ease, and by focusing on the potential for good, we align ourselves with opportunities for growth and success.

This aspect of the model teaches that what we say to ourselves, the stories we tell in our minds, have the power to shape our reality. A positive affirmation isn't just wishful thinking; it's a deliberate, conscious effort to rewire our brains towards resilience. It's about choosing to focus on the light at the end of the tunnel, even when surrounded by darkness. This mindset not only fuels perseverance but also creates a self-fulfilling prophecy where positivity breeds positive results.

In the MLRM, these two elements are not isolated; they are deeply interwoven into the fabric of resilience. Belief in faith and destiny provides the foundation of trust and acceptance, while the power of positive affirmation builds upon this foundation, driving forward momentum and inspiring action. Together, they form a holistic approach to resilience that is both spiritually anchored and psychologically empowering.

When faced with personal, organizational, community, or global challenges, these principles guide us to approach problems with a balanced mindset; grounded in faith, yet propelled by positivity. The MLRM encourages individuals to trust in the process, to believe that there is a purpose behind every event, and to maintain a positive outlook even in the darkest of times. It is this combination of acceptance and optimism that makes the MLRM a truly comprehensive blueprint for resilience.

By embracing these concepts, the MLRM not only aligns with ancient wisdom but also advances it by providing a structured framework that addresses the complexities of modern life. It offers practical strategies for applying these timeless principles in everyday situations, making resilience an achievable goal for everyone. This model is not just about surviving adversity; it's about thriving through it, using faith and positivity as the compass that guides us towards a resilient future.

The MLRM Framework

MLRM is built upon several key elements, each addressing a specific aspect of resilience: We've gathered these in each chapter "Chapter Gems", which serve as the cornerstones for building our resilience castle.

1. Embracing Change - Cultivating an Adaptive Mindset

- ❖ **Embrace the Uncertainty of Change**: Recognize change as a constant and develop an adaptive mindset that sees uncertainty as an opportunity for growth.

❖ **Strategic Adaptation**: Employ strategic thinking to adapt to changing circumstances while maintaining core values and objectives.

❖ **Reframe Your Perspective**: Shift from a fear-based view of change to a perspective that embraces it as a catalyst for innovation and progress.

❖ **Adaptation Over Time**: Understand that adaptation is an ongoing process, requiring continuous reflection and adjustment.

❖ **Strategic Acceptance**: Accept what cannot be changed and focus energy on areas where impact is possible.

2. Mastering Your Emotions - Building Emotional Intelligence

❖ **Emotional Regulation Through Reflection**: Use self-reflection to manage and regulate emotions, preventing them from becoming obstacles to resilience.

❖ **Patience as Emotional Mastery**: Cultivate patience as a key to mastering emotional responses, especially in the face of adversity.

❖ **Seek Divine Guidance in Emotional Turmoil**: In moments of emotional distress, seek spiritual guidance to find peace and clarity.

❖ **Restraint as Strength**: Recognize restraint as a powerful tool in managing emotions and maintaining control in difficult situations.

3. Strength in Connections - The Role of Social Support

❖ **The Power of Trusted Support Systems**: Build and maintain strong, trusted relationships that provide emotional and practical support.

❖ **Community as a Source of Strength**: Engage with community networks to create a collective resilience that is greater than the sum of its parts.

❖ **Mutual Loyalty and Trust**: Foster relationships based on mutual loyalty and trust, which are essential for enduring support.

❖ **Unity in Diversity**: Leverage the strength that comes from diverse perspectives and backgrounds within a community.

❖ **Compassionate Leadership**: Lead with compassion, recognizing the importance of empathy and understanding in fostering resilience.

❖ **Proactively Seek Alliances**: Actively seek out and build alliances that can provide support during times of crisis.

❖ **Foster Mutual Respect in Networks**: Ensure that relationships within networks are built on mutual respect, which strengthens the bonds of support.

❖ **Inclusivity as a Strategic Strength**: Embrace inclusivity as a strategy for creating resilient networks that are adaptable and robust.

4. Leading with Resilience - Organizational and Systemic Strength

❖ **Innovative Problem-Solving Under Pressure:** Cultivate the ability to think creatively and adapt quickly, especially in high-stress situations.

- ❖ **Learning from History:** Leverage historical insights to guide leadership decisions, using lessons from the past to shape the future.
- ❖ **Building Sustainable Systems:** Design systems and structures that ensure resilience and long-term sustainability, allowing organizations to thrive over time.
- ❖ **Strategic Empowerment:** Delegate responsibility effectively, fostering independent leadership and decentralized decision-making for increased agility.
- ❖ **Ethics as a Foundation:** Embed core values like fairness and justice into every facet of the organization to promote stability and trust.
- ❖ **Future-Proofing Through Planning:** Prepare for future challenges with forward-thinking strategies that ensure adaptability and crisis management.
- ❖ **Leading with Integrity:** Ground leadership in ethical principles, fostering a shared sense of purpose that strengthens the entire organization.
- ❖ **Creating a Culture of Growth:** Build an environment where innovation and learning are constant, and employees feel empowered to take risks and learn from setbacks.
- ❖ **Flexible Backup Systems:** Implement redundancy to ensure continuity in the face of disruption, maintaining operational stability when things go wrong.
- ❖ **Distributed Decision-Making:** Empower teams at all levels to make informed decisions, creating a dynamic and responsive organization.
- ❖ **Sustainable Leadership:** Model resilience and adaptability, prioritizing the well-being of both the organization and its people for long-term success.

5. Lifelong Learning - Growth Through Reflection and Education

- ❖ **Continuous Engagement with Knowledge**: Commit to lifelong learning and the continuous acquisition of knowledge as a foundation for resilience.
- ❖ **Transformational Learning Experiences**: Seek out and embrace learning experiences that challenge and transform existing perspectives.
- ❖ **Encourage and Facilitate Learning in Others**: Promote a culture of learning and reflection within communities and organizations.

6. Balance and Well-being - Nurturing the Whole Self

- ❖ **Holistic Well-Being:** Cultivate balance by integrating physical, mental, emotional, and spiritual health into everyday life through mindful practices that enhance overall resilience.
- ❖ **Moderation for Sustainability:** Practice moderation in all aspects, including diet, rest, and social interactions, to achieve a sustainable, balanced lifestyle that fosters long-term growth.
- ❖ **Mindful Practices for Resilience:** Incorporate mindfulness in daily activities, from nutrition to physical exercise, reinforcing the connection between body, mind, and spirit to build resilience.
- ❖ **Physical Activity for Strength:** Maintain regular physical exercise to support both mental and emotional well-being, ensuring a resilient foundation for life's challenges.

7. Inner Strength - Spiritual and Moral Resilience

- ❖ **Spiritual and Moral Foundations for Resilience:** Spirituality provides purpose, while moral integrity fosters consistency and well-being. Together, they reduce stress, enhance life satisfaction, and form a resilient foundation that helps navigate life's challenges with strength and grace.
- ❖ **Resilience Through Forgiveness:** Practicing forgiveness, even in the face of great wrongs, demonstrates moral strength. Letting go of grievances frees one from the weight of anger and fosters personal growth.
- ❖ **Spiritual Discipline for Inner Strength:** Regular spiritual practices, such as prayer and reflection, cultivate inner strength, preparing individuals to face adversity with a calm and steady heart.
- ❖ **Patience and Trust in Divine Wisdom:** Accepting loss and setbacks with patience, while maintaining faith in a higher wisdom, strengthens one's ability to endure hardships with resilience.
- ❖ **Ethical Decision-Making and Inclusivity:** Moral resilience also involves seeking justice and inclusivity in decision-making, valuing diverse perspectives, and upholding ethical principles.

8. Strengthening the Body - The Role of Physical Health

- ❖ **Physical Activity as a Foundation of Resilience**: Recognize physical health as a key component of resilience and engage in regular physical activity.
- ❖ **Healthy Habits and Regular Hygiene**: Develop and maintain healthy habits and keep regular

hygiene practices that support long-term physical well-being.

❖ **Lead by Example in Physical Effort**: Demonstrate resilience through physical effort and discipline, setting an example for others.

9. Navigating New Horizons – Embracing Change and Innovation. (for now, it is digital, who knows what next, keep open minded)

❖ **Navigating New Horizons**: Embracing Innovation and Change. True resilience is about embracing new opportunities, adapting to evolving challenges, and proactively seeking growth in all aspects of life.

❖ **Digital Resilience:** In today's tech-driven world, resilience means adapting to digital changes, protecting mental health, and maintaining thoughtful online interactions.

❖ **Purposeful Communication:** Engage in clear, value-driven digital communication to foster resilience, just as strategic communication was key in historical leadership.

❖ **Critical Thinking:** Navigate information overload by applying critical thinking, safeguarding against misinformation and digital threats.

❖ **Delegation in the Digital Age:** Focus on your strengths and delegate tasks to manage digital complexities effectively, ensuring sustained productivity and resilience.

❖ **Mastery of Digital Tools:** Master communication tools, using them wisely to strengthen your presence in virtual environments.

❖ **Data Protection:** Protect personal information and ensure the credibility of digital content, paralleling the safeguarding of knowledge in traditional systems.

10. Financial Freedom - Achieving Economic Resilience

- ❖ **Financial Stability:** Essential for reducing stress, enabling long-term planning, and fostering personal growth.
- ❖ **Impact of Financial Stress:** Recognize the significant toll of financial stress on mental, emotional, and physical well-being, highlighting the need for resilience.
- ❖ **Ethical Financial Practices:** Building trust and achieving long-term success require honesty, integrity, and fairness in financial dealings.
- ❖ **Fair Trade and Wealth Distribution:** Promote equitable financial transactions to create a more resilient and just community.
- ❖ **Avoiding Exploitation:** Adhere to ethical principles, such as avoiding usury, to maintain economic stability and resilience.
- ❖ **Trust and Contentment:** Embrace a mindset of sufficiency and gratitude, understanding that true financial freedom comes from contentment, not just wealth.
- ❖ **Equitable Distribution:** Ensure fairness in resource allocation, as demonstrated by managing wealth equitably, which strengthens overall economic resilience.
- ❖ **Proactive Crisis Management:** Prepare for financial uncertainties by setting aside savings and proactively planning to handle unexpected challenges.

11. Strength in Unity - Fostering Collective and Global Resilience

* **Collective Resilience:** Build strength through shared purpose, resource pooling, and unified support networks.
* **Global Cooperation:** Foster resilience by uniting communities to address shared global challenges.
* **Shared Responsibility:** Create lasting resilience by embracing collective accountability within communities.
* **Unified Purpose:** Harness the power of a shared vision to strengthen and unify diverse groups.
* **Global Brotherhood:** Promote equality and inclusivity for a global community that thrives in times of crisis.
* **Inclusive Policies:** Protect and empower all members of society to cultivate a resilient, harmonious collective.
* **Trust and Consultation:** Build trust and emotional security through inclusive decision-making and support.

12. Stories of Strength - Learning from Real-Life Resilience

* **Perseverance in Adversity:** True resilience is about facing challenges with unwavering determination, not avoiding them. Perseverance, rooted in faith and purpose, is the foundation of inner strength.
* **Compassion Leadership Through Resilience:** Leadership marked by mercy, compassion, unity, and strategic decision-making

during crises highlights how resilient leaders shape the future.

* **Supportive Relationships:** Strong, supportive relationships provide emotional strength, helping us navigate hardships with greater resilience.
* **Faith as a Source of Strength:** Belief in a higher purpose, as demonstrated in stories of faith, sustains individuals through even the most severe challenges.
* **Forgiveness as Inner Strength:** The ability to forgive, even when wronged, requires immense inner resilience and contributes to greater emotional freedom and strength.
* **Sacrifice for Higher Purpose:** Resilience often requires sacrifice, as seen in the willingness to undertake difficult journeys for the sake of a higher goal.
* **Courage in Adversity:** Standing firm in your convictions, even when faced with immense pressure, is a hallmark of resilience.
* **Endurance in Exile:** Resilience is not just about survival but thriving in adversity. Maintaining faith and unity through hardship fosters lasting endurance.

13. Future-Proofing Your Resilience - Preparing for Tomorrow's Challenges

* **Anticipating Future Threats:** Proactively identify potential disruptions and develop strategies to mitigate them before they arise.
* **Building Strategic Alliances:** Forge strong partnerships across industries and cultures to enhance resilience in navigating uncertainties.

- ❖ **Empowering Through Education:** Invest in continuous learning and skill development to prepare individuals and societies for future complexities.
- ❖ **Proactive Infrastructure Planning:** Establish physical, technological, and organizational structures early to support future growth.
- ❖ **Inclusive Leadership:** Engage diverse perspectives to foster collaboration and resolve conflicts, thereby strengthening future-ready resilience.
- ❖ **Long-Term Vision in Governance and Leadership:** Develop a sustainable, long-term vision that empowers future generations to thrive and grow.

The Edge of MLRM Against Other Theories

In the ever-evolving landscape of resilience studies, numerous theories have emerged, each contributing valuable insights into how individuals, organizations, and societies can withstand and grow from adversity. Among these, the MLRM stands out, not merely as a new entrant but as a comprehensive, advanced framework that aligns with and surpasses existing theories. MLRM's unique integration of moral, spiritual, emotional, psychological, social, and community resilience positions it as a superior model, addressing gaps in traditional approaches and offering a more holistic path to resilience across personal, organizational, community, and global levels.

Alignment with Existing Theories

1. **Resilience Theory (Ecological Systems Theory)**: Bronfenbrenner's Ecological Systems Theory, which forms the backbone of modern resilience theory, emphasizes the interaction between individuals and their various environments; micro, meso, exo, and macrosystems. MLRM aligns with this by recognizing that resilience is not developed in isolation. Instead, it is nurtured within a complex web of relationships, environments, and societal norms.

MLRM's Edge: While the Ecological Systems Theory is primarily descriptive, MLRM goes further by prescribing actionable steps across moral, spiritual, emotional, and social dimensions. It integrates the ecological perspective into its pillars, ensuring that resilience is cultivated not only by external systems but also through internal moral and ethical grounding, as inspired by the life of Prophet Muhammad.

2. **Resilience as a Trait and Process (Masten's Ordinary Magic)**: Ann Masten's concept of "Ordinary Magic" emphasizes that resilience arises from everyday processes and interactions. MLRM supports this view by showcasing how the Prophet Muhammad's life embodied resilience through everyday actions and decisions, such as his commitment to ethical business practices, social justice, and personal discipline.

MLRM's Edge: MLRM builds on "Ordinary Magic" by introducing a spiritual dimension, arguing that resilience is not just about ordinary processes but also about an extraordinary connection with a higher purpose. This adds depth to Masten's theory, highlighting that resilience is also about aligning one's life with moral and ethical principles, which can provide a stronger foundation for enduring adversity.

3. **Adaptive Capacity and Transformative Resilience (Walker and Holling's Adaptive Cycle)**: The Adaptive Cycle, proposed by Walker and Holling, describes resilience as the ability to adapt and transform in the face of challenges. MLRM aligns with this by emphasizing adaptability and transformation in its Emotional and Psychological Resilience pillar, where individuals are encouraged to process emotions, learn from experiences, and grow stronger.

MLRM's Edge: MLRM enhances this concept by integrating spiritual and moral dimensions, which provide additional layers of support and guidance during the adaptive process. It argues that true transformation occurs not only through psychological adaptation but also through moral integrity and spiritual growth, making it a more comprehensive approach.

4. **Resilience and Positive Psychology (Seligman's PERMA Model)**: Seligman's PERMA Model focuses on positive emotions, engagement, relationships, meaning, and accomplishment as key components of well-being and resilience. MLRM aligns with this by emphasizing similar components in its Emotional and Psychological Resilience pillar.

MLRM's Edge: MLRM surpasses the PERMA Model by integrating these elements into a framework that is deeply rooted in ethical and spiritual practices. For instance, while

PERMA emphasizes meaning, MLRM grounds meaning in a higher moral and spiritual purpose, inspired by the Prophet Muhammad's life. This provides a more robust foundation for resilience, especially in the face of existential challenges.

5. **Community Resilience (Norris et al.'s Four-Phase Model)**: The Four-Phase Model of community resilience outlines a process that communities go through in response to disasters: preparedness, response, recovery, and mitigation. MLRM complements this model by emphasizing the role of Social and Community Resilience, advocating for proactive community building, ethical leadership, and collective action as essential components of resilience.

MLRM's Edge: MLRM adds a critical moral and spiritual layer to community resilience, arguing that true collective strength arises not just from practical preparedness but from a shared commitment to ethical principles and mutual support. This spiritual and moral foundation strengthens community bonds and enhances the ability to respond to and recover from adversity.

Why MLRM is Superior and Should Be Adopted

1. **Holistic Approach**: While most resilience models focus on psychological, social, or community aspects, MLRM integrates all dimensions; moral, ethical, spiritual, emotional, and social. This comprehensive approach cultivates resilience across all areas of life, addressing the often-overlooked inner dimensions and providing a complete and sustainable solution.

2. **Actionable Framework**: Many theories are descriptive, but MLRM offers prescriptive, actionable steps inspired by the life of Prophet Muhammad. This makes it a practical tool that individuals, organizations, and communities can apply in real-world contexts.

3. **Universality and Timelessness**: Rooted in the universal principles demonstrated by the Prophet Muhammad, MLRM transcends cultural and temporal boundaries. Its timeless wisdom is relevant for today's challenges and adaptable to future uncertainties.

4. **Moral and Ethical Foundation**: In a world often plagued by ethical lapses, MLRM's emphasis on moral resilience stands out. It teaches that true resilience is about surviving adversity while upholding values like integrity, justice, and compassion.

5. **Future-Proofing Resilience**: MLRM is forward-looking, designed to adapt to future challenges, from technological shifts to global crises. It encourages continuous growth and evolution, making resilience not just about bouncing back, but thriving.

The Market and Academic Value of MLRM

- **Market Relevance**: MLRM is versatile, suitable for industries ranging from corporate resilience strategies to community development. Its focus on ethical leadership aligns with the growing demand for values-driven business practices.

- **Academic Potential**: MLRM offers a multidimensional framework for academic exploration in psychology, sociology, business ethics, and global studies, opening new research avenues on moral, spiritual, and psychological resilience.

- **Addresses Gaps**: Unlike models that focus solely on emotional intelligence or leadership, MLRM fills gaps by addressing spiritual, moral, and community dimensions of resilience.

Final Thoughts

The Legacy of Resilience

The Choice is Yours!

We live in an upside-down world where the loudest voices often belong to those with the least wisdom. Celebrities who contribute little more than entertainment have become our modern idols; actors, athletes, and singers who, through vulgarity, controversy, or mindless entertainment, rake in millions and control markets. They command attention not by virtue of intelligence, character, or contribution, but by exploiting the shallow desires of a society that has grown numb to real substance.

It's as if fame and fortune have become the rewards for the least thoughtful among us, a bizarre phenomenon where those who swear the loudest and disrespect the most are somehow celebrated. Meanwhile, the real heroes; the innovators, the thinkers, the silent builders of progress; are overlooked, marginalized, and even ridiculed. We've exchanged wisdom for spectacle, and in doing so, we've lost touch with what it means to truly lead, inspire, and change the world.

The truth is, the world is starving for real role models. The kind of heroes who build civilizations, not just entertain them. Leaders who inspire not by shock value or shallow performance, but by their unwavering dedication to something larger than themselves. Figures who remind us that true greatness isn't measured by followers or paychecks, but by the impact one leaves on humanity. Yet, they remain in the shadows, overshadowed by the noise of those who contribute nothing but fleeting distraction.

We've mistaken noise for progress, forgetting that the world doesn't change because someone made a crowd laugh or filled a stadium. It changes because someone had the courage to stand for something meaningful, to defy the status quo, and to build something lasting. What we need are thinkers, builders, and doers; not performers chasing the next viral moment.

The future depends on the heroes we choose to celebrate. Will we continue to worship the trivial and the transient? Or will we rise up and demand a new standard for who we hold up as our icons? The choice is ours. And until we make it, the fools will continue to rule, and the true leaders will remain in the shadows.

What's worse is the impact this has on those who stand for something true and meaningful. We've reached a point where those who uphold integrity and wisdom are made to doubt themselves. Surrounded by the overwhelming confidence of those who promote falsehood, the right begin to wonder if they're the crazy ones. After all, how can so many be so wrong and yet so certain? How can impudence parade as truth, while humility and decency are questioned, mocked, and marginalized?

This is the reality we face today: a world where those who shout the loudest; often with nothing of value to say; command the attention, while those with true insight and moral conviction are drowned out. It's a dangerous trend, because when the truth is pushed to the margins, society suffers. The people who could lead us to a better future are made to question their sanity, their vision, even their worth.

But this is where the power of choice comes in. You can be swayed by the loud, the flashy, the shallow, and be carried along in a current of mediocrity and falsehood. Or you can choose to walk the path of the greats, the ones who didn't seek attention but built something real, something lasting. You can become a leader in your own right, not by following the crowd, but by standing firm in the face of a world gone mad with false idols.

The truth may be drowned out for a time, but it never disappears. It remains, steady, waiting for those with the courage to seek it out. The choice is yours: will you settle for the hollow echoes of today's false icons, or will you rise above, seeking the wisdom, strength, and resilience of true leaders?

Remember the Story About the Jewish Man?!

And now my thoughts on the story of Prophet Muhammad pawning his shield to a Jewish man, rather than seeking help from his wealthy companions, reveals layers of wisdom and deliberate choices. Here's why:

1. Self-Reliance Over Dependency

Even as the leader of a growing community, Prophet Muhammad embodied personal responsibility. He chose not to burden others, reinforcing that self-reliance is a key principle of resilience. This wasn't a denial of his companions' generosity, but a model of how even leaders should carry their own weight.

2. Humility in Leadership

Despite having wealthy companions like Uthman and Abdur-Rahman ibn Awf, the Prophet avoided any special treatment. By pawning his shield, he demonstrated that true leadership isn't about accessing privilege but living humbly, even in hardship.

3. Equality and Fairness

The Prophet's decision ensured that none of his companions felt obligated to support him financially. By engaging in a simple transaction with a Jewish man, he showed that wealth and status should never influence fairness or relationships within a community.

4. Interfaith Trust and Coexistence

This act wasn't just about personal finances; it was a powerful statement on trust and cooperation across religious boundaries. The Prophet demonstrated that resilience includes building bridges and treating everyone, regardless of faith, with respect and fairness.

5. Ethical Resilience

The Prophet's actions highlighted ethical resilience. Even in moments of need, he maintained his integrity, showing that real resilience involves meeting challenges head-on without compromising personal values or burdening others.

To be fair; the more I delve into the life of Muhammad, the more I find myself in awe of him. He operates on an entirely different level. Any reasonable person with a fair mind and authentic, natural clarity of thought can't help but admire him. His wisdom, character, and resilience are truly remarkable.

The most touching piece I've read about him is a poem by Hassan ibn Thabit, one of his companions. It beautifully illustrates the profound love and admiration his companions had for him and how positively he impacted their lives. They were willing to protect him with everything they had, loving him more than anything else in the world. And my humble translation of his poem goes as below

> *My eyes have never seen a soul so true,*
> *No woman birthed a beauty like you.*
> *In form and grace, you have no flaw,*
> *As if you shaped yourself by your own law.*

Muhammad (PBUH) as the Archetype of Resilience

But hold on, Muhammad's existence predates any formal resilience theories. Could he be the original source of all resilience concepts? Let's delve deeper.

This claim holds a compelling argument, especially when we look at the unique position of Prophet Muhammad (PBUH) and how his life offers a holistic model of resilience that predates modern theories. The notion that the MLRM encapsulates the core elements of resilience long before they were formalized into psychological, social, or leadership frameworks is both intriguing and defensible. Here's a breakdown of the reasoning behind the claim:

1. Timeless Foundations of Resilience

The Prophet's life offers timeless examples of resilience; whether moral, spiritual, emotional, or social; that modern theories of resilience later attempt to categorize and formalize. Concepts like *shura* (consultation), *tawakkul* (trust in destiny), and long-term strategic thinking resonate with what we now recognize as essential to resilience: adaptability, foresight, and community support.

2. The Precedent of MLRM's Core Pillars

MLRM's pillars, like Moral and Ethical Resilience, Spiritual Resilience, Emotional and Psychological Resilience, and Social and Community Resilience, are already complete frameworks in their own right. These align with, and often go beyond, modern theories in comprehensiveness and depth. For instance, modern psychology emphasizes the role of meaning-making and positive mindset in resilience, but Muhammad's life showed an even deeper, spiritually anchored resilience long before these concepts were articulated in psychology.

3. Muhammad's Life: A Source of Resilience Theories

Muhammad's existence preceded every major modern theory of resilience, and the strategies he employed; like consultation, strategic foresight, and ethical leadership; are mirrored in contemporary frameworks like Cognitive Behavioral Therapy (CBT), systems thinking, and adaptive leadership models. This allows for the argument that MLRM isn't just another model; it's *the* source model from which many principles of resilience are derived.

4. Authenticity and Universality

The fact that Muhammad's life was documented with precision adds authenticity to the claim. His model isn't speculative; it's a lived example with a proven track record across personal, social, and organizational resilience. As Muhammad (PBUH) was influencing nearly every aspect of life; from personal well-being to state-building; the MLRM reflects a holistic theory of resilience that anticipates later fragmented theories, which only touch on individual aspects like emotional or social resilience.

5. Bridging Ancient Wisdom with Modern Thought

One of the most compelling aspects of this claim is that it bridges ancient wisdom with modern resilience thought. Rather than seeing resilience as a modern construct, MLRM presents it as a universal principle that has always existed, with Muhammad (PBUH) being the foremost exemplar. It brings forward the idea that many of the strategies and techniques we now consider "modern" were, in essence, practiced centuries ago under Muhammad's leadership.

Therefore; the Prophet Muhammad (PBUH) isn't just a historical figure who demonstrated resilience, but rather the archetype and source of resilience itself. He was so remarkably perfect that you can't help but acknowledge he was guided by a divine force. His life laid out the very foundations that all future resilience theories would merely formalize and categorize. In this view, MLRM doesn't merely align with modern theories; it transcends and predates them, offering a blueprint from which all others are derived.

Why Resilience not Resistance?!

In the psychology market, *resilience* and *resistance* are often misunderstood as interchangeable terms, but they lead to dramatically different outcomes in the face of adversity. MLRM emphasizes resilience over resistance, and for good reason.

- Resistance is about pushing back against challenges, often with rigidity and refusal to adapt. While resistance can offer short-term protection, it tends to drain energy and leaves little room for growth. It's like standing firm in a storm; while you may stay rooted for a time, you're eventually worn down by external forces.

- Resilience, on the other hand, is about flexibility and adaptation. MLRM teaches that resilience means not only withstanding the storm but using it to grow stronger. Like a tree that bends with the wind, resilience allows for recovery and development even after significant challenges. It promotes long-term growth, allowing individuals and organizations to evolve and thrive.

In the psychology market, resilience is the superior concept because it fosters growth and transformation. Resistance may help in momentary battles, but resilience wins the war by cultivating adaptability, strength, and long-term well-being.

the Prophet Muhammad (PBUH) demonstrated *resistance* when it was necessary for short-term gains, and this aspect is represented in the MLRM. However, what sets him apart is his ability to know when to resist and when to be resilient.

Resistance for Strategic Gains: The Prophet mastered resistance when it served a greater purpose. For example, during the *early Meccan period*, he and his followers resisted immense persecution without retaliation. This wasn't passive submission but a calculated resistance that allowed the Muslim community to grow in strength and numbers. Another instance is the *Battle of the Trench*, where they resisted the enemies' attack by adopting a defensive strategy. Resistance was used as a tactical pause to conserve energy and secure a stronger position.

The element of resistance in the MLRM is woven into its focus on *moral and ethical resilience*. It reflects the idea that sometimes-standing firm in the face of immediate pressure is necessary to maintain one's values and strategic objectives. But it's always a means to an end, not the end itself. The model acknowledges that resistance, when aligned with long-term goals, can create the conditions for resilience and growth.

So, while resistance is part of the model, it's always viewed as a temporary strategy; a bridge to resilience. MLRM teaches that knowing when to resist and when to adapt is what leads to true mastery over life's challenges.

MLRM embodies resilience at its core, showing that true success comes not just from enduring hardship, but from using those challenges as opportunities for growth and personal evolution.

By focusing on resilience rather than resistance, MLRM prepares individuals, organizations, and communities not just to survive but to thrive in the face of life's uncertainties.

As we are approaching the end of this book, remember that the journey of resilience is far from over; it's just beginning. The lessons you've absorbed, the stories that have resonated with you, and the principles of the MLRM are not just tools for today; they are the building blocks for a future defined by strength, adaptability, and enduring legacy.

Ongoing Journey: The Lifelong Path of Resilience

Resilience is not a finish line you cross with a sigh of relief. It's not a state of being that you achieve and then rest upon. Resilience is a dynamic process, a constant evolution. It's about facing each new challenge with the wisdom gleaned from the past and the courage to adapt for the future. Just as Prophet Muhammad's life was a series of tests and triumphs, each of us is on a journey where every obstacle is an opportunity to grow stronger, wiser, and more compassionate.

Think back to the stories we've explored; the Prophet's strategic foresight during the Battle of Tabuk, the long-term vision enshrined in the Medina Constitution, and the simple yet profound act of planting a tree even when the end of the world is imminent. These stories aren't just historical anecdotes; they are blueprints for how to approach life's challenges. They remind us that resilience is built not in the absence of adversity but in the very heart of it. Every setback, every trial, every moment of uncertainty is a chance to fortify your resolve and continue moving forward.

A Lasting Impact: Crafting a Legacy of Resilience

The MLRM framework, inspired by the timeless wisdom of Prophet Muhammad, is more than a guide for personal growth; it's a roadmap for creating a legacy of resilience that will echo through generations. By integrating moral, ethical, spiritual, emotional, psychological, and social resilience into your life, you're not just preparing yourself for the future; you're shaping the future for others.

Consider the impact of your actions today. The way you navigate challenges, the values you uphold, the compassion you extend to others; all of these contribute to the legacy you leave behind. The Prophet's life teaches us that true resilience is not self-contained; it radiates outward, touching the lives of others and creating a ripple effect that can change the world. Your journey doesn't end with personal success; it continues through the influence you have on your community, your family, and the broader world.

Imagine future generations drawing strength from the examples you set. Picture them finding guidance in the resilience you built, the ethical standards you upheld, and the compassion you showed in difficult times. This is the lasting impact of resilience; it's not just about surviving; it's about thriving in a way that leaves the world better than you found it.

The Legacy You're Building

As you step back into your life, armed with the insights and strategies you've gathered, remember that resilience is your legacy. It's the enduring strength you pass on to those who come after you. It's the wisdom that guides you through the unknown and the courage that carries you when the path is steep.

The legacy of resilience is not written in grand gestures but in the small, consistent choices you make every day. It's in the way you respond to adversity, the way you uplift others, and the way you remain true to your values, no matter the cost.

As you continue your journey, keep the principles of the MLRM close. Let them guide you as you navigate the challenges ahead, and let them inspire you to build a future where resilience is not just a personal trait but a collective strength. The story of your resilience is still being written, and its final chapter is far from complete. Each day is a new opportunity to add to that story, to build a legacy that will stand the test of time.

So go forth with confidence, with purpose, and with the unshakable belief that resilience is not just your birthright; it's your gift to the world.

The Book Cover

The painting captures a powerful and textured landscape, rich with symbolism for resilience. At the top, a towering mountainous terrain is illuminated by a large, bright full moon. This moon reflects the way Prophet Muhammad, peace be upon him, was often described by his companions; like the full moon, radiant and unreachable, embodying his ability to overcome all adversity. It's a visual metaphor for his resilience, surmounting obstacles and rising above challenges.

On the right, waves crash against rocks, a timeless symbol of resilience itself; persistence meeting resistance, and yet continuing on with unwavering determination. This image echoes the relentless nature of resilience in the face of hardship.

On the left side, which spans the back cover, wavy lines in blue and beige represent the fluidity of water and sand, symbolizing the continuous ebb and flow of challenges. The sandy color symbolizes the Arabian Peninsula, where Muhammad was born and raised. A vertical line divides the image, contrasting the soft textures and colors on the left with the darker, more defined lines on the right. This juxtaposition mirrors the balance between moderation and resistance; between fluidly navigating life's uncertainties and standing firm when met with trials.

Through these natural elements; water's adaptability, the mountain's enduring strength, and the wave's persistence; the image visually embodies the core qualities of resilience: the ability to endure, adapt, and persevere against the forces of adversity.

Appendices: Tools for Your Resilience Journey

As we move from the insights shared in the main chapters, this section is crafted to be your personal toolkit for the journey ahead. We've gathered everything from our chapters and put it in one place to make it more handy for you. Consider it your map, compass, and gear for navigating the unpredictable terrain of life with unshakeable resilience. We've explored the profound lessons derived from the Prophet Muhammad's life, woven them into the MLRM, and now, we're arming you with practical tools to apply these principles to your everyday life.

This appendix is your interactive guide; a hands-on companion that transforms knowledge into action. Whether you're seeking to deepen your understanding, reflect on your experiences, or actively build your resilience, these tools are here to support you every step of the way.

Practical Exercises and Reflections: Building Your Resilience Muscle

Resilience isn't just something you learn; it's something you practice. The following exercises are designed to strengthen your resilience through deliberate practice and self-reflection. Each exercise targets one of the four pillars of the MLRM, ensuring that you build a well-rounded, robust resilience.

1. Moral and Ethical Resilience: Aligning Actions with Values

- **Exercise:** Values in Action
    - o **Step 1**: List your top five core values. These might include honesty, compassion, justice, or any other principles you hold dear.
    - o **Step 2**: Reflect on a recent decision or action you took. Did it align with your listed values? If not, how could you have approached it differently?
    - o **Step 3**: Commit to making one decision this week that consciously aligns with your core values. Document the outcome and how it made you feel.
- **Reflection Prompt**: "How does living in alignment with my values enhance my resilience? What challenges do I face in staying true to my values, and how can I overcome them?"

2. Spiritual Resilience: Deepening Your Connection

- **Exercise:** Daily Mindfulness and Prayer
    - o **Step 1**: Set aside 10 minutes each day for a mindfulness or prayer session. Focus on your breathing, a meaningful phrase, or a spiritual passage.
    - o **Step 2**: After the session, write down any insights or feelings that arise. How does this practice ground you?

- Step 3: Identify one spiritual practice (like gratitude, forgiveness, or charity) that you can incorporate into your daily routine. Observe its impact on your sense of inner peace and resilience.
- **Reflection Prompt**: "In what ways does my spiritual practice serve as a source of strength in difficult times? How can I deepen this practice to enhance my resilience?"

3. Emotional and Psychological Resilience: Mastering Your Inner World

- **Exercise:** Emotional Regulation Journal
    - Step 1: For one week, track your emotional responses to various situations in a journal. Note the trigger, your initial reaction, and how you managed it.
    - Step 2: Identify patterns. Are there specific triggers that consistently provoke a strong reaction? What alternative strategies could you use to respond more effectively?
    - Step 3: Choose one emotional regulation technique (such as deep breathing, cognitive reframing, or pausing before reacting) to practice in moments of stress. Document the results.
- **Reflection Prompt**: "How do my emotions influence my resilience? What steps can I take to ensure that my emotional responses support rather than hinder my ability to cope with challenges?"

4. Social and Community Resilience: Strengthening Connections

- **Exercise:** Building Your Support Network
    - ○ **Step 1**: List the people who are your closest supports. Consider the roles they play in your life; emotional support, practical help, or inspiration.
    - ○ **Step 2**: Reach out to each person this week, even if just to check in. Strengthen these connections through gratitude, shared activities, or simply being present.
    - ○ **Step 3**: Identify one area in your community where you can contribute. Whether through volunteering, organizing, or just showing up, take an active role in fostering community resilience.
- **Reflection Prompt**: "How does my community support my resilience? What can I do to contribute to the resilience of those around me?"

Checklists and Worksheets: Making Resilience Actionable

The following checklists and worksheets are designed to help you take the abstract concepts of resilience and translate them into concrete, actionable steps. These tools will guide you through the process of integrating the MLRM principles into your daily life, ensuring that resilience becomes a natural part of your routine.

1. Daily Resilience Checklist

- Morning
    - Start with gratitude: List three things you're grateful for today.
    - Set a daily intention: What's one thing you want to focus on today to enhance your resilience?
- Midday
    - Take a mindfulness break: Spend 5 minutes breathing or reflecting.
    - Check-in: Are you aligned with your values and intentions so far?
- Evening
    - Reflect on your day: What challenges did you face, and how did you handle them?
    - Plan for tomorrow: Identify one resilience-building action you will take.

2. Weekly Resilience Planner

- Goal Setting
    - Identify a resilience goal for the week (e.g., practice patience, deepen a spiritual practice, or strengthen a relationship).
    - Break it down: What are three specific actions you will take to achieve this goal?
- Reflection
    - At the end of the week, review your progress. What worked well? What could you improve?
    - Adjust your plan for the next week based on what you've learned.

3. Resilience Assessment Worksheet

- Self-Assessment
  - ○ Rate yourself on a scale of 1-5 in each of the four MLRM pillars: Moral and Ethical Resilience, Spiritual Resilience, Emotional and Psychological Resilience, and Social and Community Resilience.
  - ○ Identify strengths and areas for growth. Where are you strongest? Where could you use more focus?
- Action Plan
  - ○ Choose one area to focus on for the next month. What specific steps will you take to strengthen this aspect of your resilience?
  - ○ Set a date to reassess and adjust your plan as needed.

Resources for Further Study: Deepening Your Understanding

The journey of resilience is one of continuous learning. The more you understand, the more tools you have at your disposal to face life's challenges with confidence and strength. If you're eager to enhance your understanding of resilience, my reference list is packed with valuable resources. These materials; ranging from books and articles to online resources; will offer you deeper insights into resilience, both within the MLRM framework and beyond. Whether you're looking to explore spiritual, emotional, or community-based resilience, you'll find a wealth of knowledge that can help you face life's challenges with strength and confidence.

But believe me when I say this: MLRM is already the distilled essence of all these readings. I've spent years diving deep into these concepts, researching, and refining them, and I genuinely believe that the Muhammad's Lasting Resilience Model captures it all. If there's anything I might have missed, it's simply due to human error or forgetfulness; not because the model lacks in any way.

If you're looking for engaging online tools, check out these resources

Some Online Hub Resources

- **"The Resilience Center"**: An online hub offering courses, articles, and community forums dedicated to building resilience.
- **"Mindful"**: A resource for mindfulness practices that support emotional and psychological resilience.
- **"The Global Resilience Partnership"**: An organization focused on enhancing resilience on a global scale, particularly in vulnerable communities.

Reflection:

- **Interactive Engagement**: These appendices are designed to be hands-on, encouraging active participation in your resilience journey through practical exercises, checklists, and reflection prompts.
- **Action-Oriented Tools**: The checklists and worksheets provide a structured approach to integrating the MLRM principles into your daily life, making resilience actionable and measurable.
- **Continual Learning**: The resources for further study offer a path for deepening your understanding

of resilience, ensuring that your journey doesn't end here but continues to evolve and grow.

Acknowledgments

First and foremost, I express my deepest gratitude to Allah, the Most Gracious, the Most Merciful. His guidance and blessings have been the cornerstone of this journey. In moments of doubt and challenge, His infinite wisdom has provided clarity and strength.

I also extend my heartfelt thanks to Prophet Muhammad (PBUH). His teachings and exemplary life have been a source of profound wisdom and moral guidance. The principles he embodied have shaped my values and provided a framework for navigating life's complexities.

Lastly, I would like to extend my gratitude to the various tools and technologies that supported me throughout the writing of this book. In particular, I acknowledge the assistance of AI, which helped refine ideas, draft content, and bring clarity to some complex topics. This technology has been a valuable companion in aiding in the creative process.

Here are my modest words in his praise.

In desert sands where tempests rise,
And truth was veiled by shadowed skies,
A soul emerged, divinely bright,
To guide the lost through darkest night.

Muhammad stood, a pillar tall,
When nations trembled, doomed to fall,
With every trial, every storm,
He kept his heart, his spirit warm.

An orphaned child, yet never frail,
He faced the world without a veil.
Adversity his daily bread,
But from the path, he never fled.

Through battles fought with courage pure,
His soul remained both firm and sure.
He sought no vengeance, sought no fame,
Yet history still reveres his name.

Resilience carved in every deed,
He planted hope in times of need.
His moral strength, a beacon's glow,
That taught the world which way to go.

No wealth he asked, no riches sought,
His peace was found in all he taught.
A shield he pawned, not for his gain,
But so his word might still remain.

He is the model, perfect, whole,
A guide for every searching soul.
By Divine hand, his steps were led,
A flame of hope where all else bled.

Muhammad, though my words may fall too shy,
I speak, for your example lifts me high.
Each praise I give is but a humble sign,
Yet in your grace, you make each word shine.

The more I praise, the higher still I rise,
For Allah guides us through your noble ties.
You are the mirror of what humankind could be,
The model for all hearts that seek to see.

Dr. Ashi Ezz

To follow you, the greatest aim we find,
For in your steps, we leave our doubts behind.
Muhammad's path, a journey ever true,
A map for hearts to seek and then renew.

References

Ainsworth, M. D. S., & Bowlby, J. (1991). An ethological approach to personality development. Cambridge University Press.

Al-Jazuli, M. (2007). Dalail al-Khayrat. Dar Al Kotob Al Ilmiyah.

Al-Mubarakpuri, S. (1996). Ar-Raheeq Al-Makhtum (The Sealed Nectar): Biography of the Noble Prophet (Revised Edition). Dar-us-Salam Publications.

Al-Samarkandi, A. H. (1998). Kitab al-Samarkandiyya. Dar al-Minhaj.

Al-Tirmidhi, M. I. (2008). Al-Shamā'il al-Muhammadiyya (A. Bewley, Trans.). Diwan Press.

Al-Yahsubi, Q. A. (2003). Ash-Shifa bi Ta'rif Huquq al-Mustafa (A. Bewley, Trans.). Madinah Press.

Antonovsky, A. (1987). Unraveling the mystery of health: How people manage stress and stay well. Jossey-Bass.

Avey, J. B., Luthans, F., Smith, R. M., & Palmer, N. F. (2010). Impact of positive psychological capital on employee well-being over time. Journal of Occupational Health Psychology, 15(1), 17–28.

Bandura, A. (1997). Self-efficacy: The exercise of control. W. H. Freeman.

Bandura, A. (2001). Social cognitive theory: An agentic perspective. Annual Review of Psychology, 52(1), 1-26.

Bar-On, R. (2006). The Bar-On model of emotional-social intelligence (ESI). Psicothema, 18, 13-25.

Baumeister, R. F., & Leary, M. R. (1995). The need to belong: Desire for interpersonal attachments as a fundamental human motivation. Psychological Bulletin, 117(3), 497-529.

Baumeister, R. F., & Tierney, J. (2011). Willpower: Rediscovering the greatest human strength. Penguin Press.

Beck, A. T. (1993). Cognitive therapy: Past, present, and future. Journal of Consulting and Clinical Psychology, 61(2), 194-198.

Beck, A. T., & Freeman, A. (1990). Cognitive therapy of personality disorders. Guilford Press.

Block, J. H., & Block, J. (1980). The role of ego-control and ego-resiliency in the organization of behavior. In W. A. Collins (Ed.), Minnesota symposium on child psychology, 13, 39-101.

Bonanno, G. A. (2004). Loss, trauma, and human resilience: Have we underestimated the human capacity to thrive after extremely aversive events? American Psychologist, 59(1), 20-28.

Brown, K. W., & Ryan, R. M. (2003). The benefits of being present: Mindfulness and its role in psychological well-being. Journal of Personality and Social Psychology, 84(4), 822–848.

Bukhari, M. I. (1997). *Sahih Bukhari* (M. M. Khan, Trans.). Dar-us-Salam Publications.

Carver, C. S. (1997). You want to measure coping but your protocol's too long: Consider the brief COPE. International Journal of Behavioral Medicine, 4(1), 92-100.

Carver, C. S., & Scheier, M. F. (1998). On the self-regulation of behavior. Cambridge University Press.

Charney, D. S. (2004). Psychobiological mechanisms of resilience and vulnerability: Implications for successful adaptation to extreme stress. American Journal of Psychiatry, 161(2), 195-216.

Charney, D. S., & Southwick, S. M. (2012). Resilience: The science of mastering life's greatest challenges. Cambridge University Press.

Cloninger, C. R. (2004). Feeling good: The science of well-being. Journal of Affective Disorders, 78(2), 205-215.

Covey, S. R. (1989). The 7 habits of highly effective people: Powerful lessons in personal change. Free Press.

Csikszentmihalyi, M. (1990). Flow: The psychology of optimal experience. Harper & Row.

Csikszentmihalyi, M. (1996). Creativity: Flow and the psychology of discovery and invention. HarperPerennial.

Deci, E. L., & Ryan, R. M. (2000). The "what" and "why" of goal pursuits: Human needs and the self-determination of behavior. Psychological Inquiry, 11(4), 227-268.

Diener, E., & Oishi, S. (2000). Money and happiness: Income and subjective well-being across nations. Culture and subjective well-being (pp. 185-218). MIT Press.

Diener, E., & Seligman, M. E. P. (2002). Very happy people. Psychological Science, 13(1), 81-84.

Duckworth, A. (2016). Grit: The power of passion and perseverance. Scribner.

Duckworth, A. L., & Gross, J. J. (2014). Self-control and grit: Related but separable determinants of success. Current Directions in Psychological Science, 23(5), 319-325.

Duhigg, C. (2012). The power of habit: Why we do what we do in life and business. Random House.

Dweck, C. S. (2006). Mindset: The new psychology of success. Random House.

Dweck, C. S., & Leggett, E. L. (1988). A social-cognitive approach to motivation and personality. Psychological Review, 95(2), 256-273.

Eisenberger, R., & Rhoades, L. (2002). Perceived organizational support: A review of the literature. Journal of Applied Psychology, 87(4), 698-714.

Erikson, E. H. (1950). Childhood and society. W. W. Norton & Company.

Folkman, S., & Moskowitz, J. T. (2000). Positive affect and the other side of coping. American Psychologist, 55(6), 647-654.

Frankl, V. E. (1959). Man's search for meaning. Beacon Press.

Fredrickson, B. L. (2001). The role of positive emotions in positive psychology: The broaden-and-build theory of positive emotions. American Psychologist, 56(3), 218–226.

Freud, S. (1923). The ego and the id. W. W. Norton & Company.

Garmezy, N. (1991). Resiliency and vulnerability to adverse developmental outcomes associated with poverty. American Behavioral Scientist, 34(4), 416-430.

Gilbert, P. (2014). The origins and nature of compassion focused therapy. British Journal of Clinical Psychology, 53(1), 6-41.

Goleman, D. (1995). Emotional intelligence: Why it can matter more than IQ. Bantam Books.

Goleman, D. (2004). Emotional intelligence: Issues in paradigm building. In P. Salovey & D. Sluyter (Eds.), Emotional development and emotional intelligence: Educational implications (pp. 13-36). Basic Books.

Hanh, T. N. (1975). The miracle of mindfulness. Beacon Press.

Hobfoll, S. E. (2001). The influence of culture, community, and the nested-self in the stress process: Advancing conservation of resources theory. Applied Psychology, 50(3), 337-370.

Ibn Hisham, A. M. (2009). Al-Sirah al-Nabawiyyah (S. Guillaume, Trans.). Oxford University Press.

Isen, A. M. (2000). Positive affect and decision making. In M. Lewis & J. M. Haviland-Jones (Eds.), Handbook of emotions (pp. 417-435). Guilford Press.

James, W. (1902). The varieties of religious experience: A study in human nature. Longmans, Green, and Co.

Kabat-Zinn, J. (1990). Full catastrophe living: Using the wisdom of your body and mind to face stress, pain, and illness. Delta.

Kabat-Zinn, J. (2003). Mindfulness-based interventions in context: Past, present, and future. Clinical Psychology: Science and Practice, 10(2), 144-156.

Kahneman, D. (2011). Thinking, fast and slow. Farrar, Straus and Giroux.

Kandhlawi, M. Z. (2004). Fada'il al-A'mal (M. A. Elias, Trans.). Kutub Khana Ishayat-ul-Islam.

Karoly, P. (1993). Mechanisms of self-regulation: A systems view. Annual Review of Psychology, 44(1), 23-52.

Kegan, R., & Lahey, L. L. (2009). Immunity to change: How to overcome it and unlock potential in yourself and your organization. Harvard Business Press.

Kotter, J. P. (1996). Leading change. Harvard Business Review Press.

Kouzes, J. M., & Posner, B. Z. (2017). The leadership challenge: How to make extraordinary things happen in organizations. Wiley.

Krishnamurti, J. (1991). Total freedom: The essential Krishnamurti. HarperOne.

Lazarus, R. S. (1993). From psychological stress to the emotions: A history of changing outlooks. Annual Review of Psychology, 44(1), 1-21.

Lazarus, R. S., & Folkman, S. (1984). Stress, appraisal, and coping. Springer.

LeDoux, J. (1996). The emotional brain: The mysterious underpinnings of emotional life. Simon & Schuster.

Locke, E. A., & Latham, G. P. (2002). Building a practically useful theory of goal setting and task motivation: A 35-year odyssey. American Psychologist.

Maslow, A. H. (1943). A theory of human motivation. Harper & Row.

Maslow, A. H. (1968). Toward a psychology of being. Van Nostrand.

Masten, A. S. (2001). Ordinary magic: Resilience processes in development. American Psychologist, 56(3), 227-238.

Masten, A. S. (2014). Ordinary magic: Resilience in development. Guilford Press.

McAdams, D. P. (2006). The redemptive self: Stories Americans live by. Oxford University Press.

McEwen, B. S., & Wingfield, J. C. (2003). The concept of allostasis in biology and biomedicine. Hormones and Behavior, 43(1), 2-15.

Miller, W. R., & Rollnick, S. (2013). Motivational interviewing: Helping people change. Guilford Press.

Neff, K. D. (2003). The development and validation of a scale to measure self-compassion. Self and Identity, 2(3), 223-250.

Pargament, K. I. (1997). The psychology of religion and coping: Theory, research, practice. Guilford Press.

Park, C. L., & Folkman, S. (1997). Meaning in the context of stress and coping. Review of General Psychology, 1(2), 115-144.

Peterson, C., & Seligman, M. E. P. (1984). Causal explanations as a risk factor for depression: Theory and evidence. Psychological Review, 91(3), 347-374.

Peterson, C., & Seligman, M. E. P. (2004). Character strengths and virtues: A handbook and classification. American Psychological Association and Oxford University Press.

Peterson, J. B. (2018). 12 rules for life: An antidote to chaos. Random House.

Porges, S. W. (2011). The polyvagal theory: Neurophysiological foundations of emotions, attachment, communication, and self-regulation. Norton & Company.

Rogers, C. R. (1961). On becoming a person: A therapist's view of psychotherapy. Houghton Mifflin.

Ross, G. R. (2014). Resilience: The science of mastering life's greatest challenges. Cambridge University Press.

Russ Harris. (2008). The happiness trap: How to stop struggling and start living. Trumpeter.

Ryff, C. D. (1989). Happiness is everything, or is it? Explorations on the meaning of psychological well-being. Journal of Personality and Social Psychology, 57(6), 1069-1081.

Ryff, C. D., & Singer, B. H. (2002). Flourishing: Positive psychology and the life well-lived. American Psychological Association.

Sapolsky, R. M. (2004). Social status and health in humans and other animals. Annual Review of Anthropology, 33(1), 393-418.

Scheier, M. F., & Carver, C. S. (1985). Optimism, coping, and health: Assessment and implications of generalized outcome expectancies. Health Psychology, 4(3), 219-247.

Schore, A. N. (2003). Early relational trauma, disorganized attachment, and the development of a predisposition to violence. In M. F. Solomon & D. J. Siegel (Eds.), Healing trauma: Attachment, mind, body, and brain (pp. 107-167). W. W. Norton.

Seligman, M. E. P. (2002). Positive psychology, positive prevention, and positive therapy. Handbook of positive psychology, 3-9.

Seligman, M. E. P. (2011). Flourish: A visionary new understanding of happiness and well-being. Free Press.

Selye, H. (1956). The stress of life. McGraw-Hill.

Dr. Ashi Ezz

Shapiro, S. L., Carlson, L. E., Astin, J. A., & Freedman, B. (2006). Mechanisms of mindfulness. Journal of Clinical Psychology, 62(3), 373-386.

Shirky, C. (2010). Cognitive surplus: Creativity and generosity in a connected age. Penguin Press.

Smith, H. (2009). The world's religions: Our great wisdom traditions. HarperOne.

Southwick, S. M., & Charney, D. S. (2012). The science of resilience: Implications for the prevention and treatment of depression. Science, 338(6103), 79-82.

Taleb, N. N. (2013). *Antifragile: Things that gain from disorder*. Penguin Books.

Tangney, J. P., Baumeister, R. F., & Boone, A. L. (2004). High self-control predicts good adjustment, less pathology, better grades, and interpersonal success. Journal of Personality, 72(2), 271-324.

Taylor, S. E. (2006). Tend and befriend: Biobehavioral bases of affiliation under stress. Current Directions in Psychological Science, 15(6), 273-277.

The Qur'an. (1999). (M. T. Al-Hilali & M. M. Khan, Trans.). King Fahd Complex for the Printing of the Holy Qur'an.

Tolle, E. (1997). The power of now: A guide to spiritual enlightenment. New World Library.

Tugade, M. M., & Fredrickson, B. L. (2004). Resilient individuals use positive emotions to bounce back from negative emotional experiences. Journal of Personality and Social Psychology, 86(2), 320-333.

Ungar, M. (2013). Resilience, trauma, context, and culture. Trauma, Violence, & Abuse, 14(3), 255-266.

Vaillant, G. E. (1993). The wisdom of the ego. Harvard University Press.

Van der Kolk, B. A. (2014). The body keeps the score: Brain, mind, and body in the healing of trauma. Viking.

Vygotsky, L. S. (1978). Mind in society: The development of higher psychological processes. Harvard University Press.

Werner, E. E., & Smith, R. S. (1992). Overcoming the odds: High-risk children from birth to adulthood. Cornell University Press.

Wilkinson, R., & Pickett, K. (2010). The spirit level: Why greater equality makes societies stronger. Bloomsbury Press.

Wolpe, J. (1969). The practice of behavior therapy. Pergamon Press.

Wright, M. O., Masten, A. S., & Narayan, A. J. (2013). Resilience processes in development: Four waves of research on positive adaptation in the context of adversity. In S. Goldstein & R. B. Brooks (Eds.), Handbook of resilience in children (pp. 15-37). Springer.

Wright, R. (1994). The moral animal: Why we are, the way we are: The new science of evolutionary psychology. Pantheon Books.

Zautra, A. J., Hall, J. S., & Murray, K. E. (2010). Resilience: A new definition of health for people and communities. In J. W. Reich, A. J. Zautra, & J. S. Hall (Eds.), Handbook of adult resilience (pp. 3-29). Guilford Press.

Zimbardo, P. G., & Boyd, J. N. (2008). The time paradox: The new psychology of time that will change your life. Simon & Schuster.

Zimmerman, M. A. (2013). Resiliency theory: A strengths-based approach to research and practice for adolescent health. Health Education & Behavior, 40(4), 381-383.

About the Author

Dr. Ashi Ezz is an expert in organizational transformation, with a doctorate specializing in risk management. Passionate about inspiring positive change, Dr. Ezz is dedicated to mentoring and coaching individuals and organizations towards better, more balanced lives. With a wealth of knowledge gained from years of practical experience, engaging with experts, and an insatiable appetite for continuous learning, Dr. Ezz is committed to empowering others to shape successful enterprises and fulfilling personal lives.

Made in the USA
Monee, IL
07 July 2026

56552289R00166